Stand~by
Unexpected lessons

Stand-by
Unexpected lessons

Ken Blackford
John Humphries

Nelson

Acknowledgements
The publishers would like to
thank William Heinemann Ltd.
for permission to use the poem
"Jargon" from *Ragged Robin* by James Reeves

The Stand-by series includes:
Stand-by   A miscellany of unexpected lessons
Stand-by 2   Fun with basic skills
Stand-by 3   Early Art and Craft

Thomas Nelson and Sons Ltd
Nelson House Mayfield Road
Walton-on-Thames Surrey
KT12 5PL UK

51 York Place
Edinburgh
EH1 3JD UK

Thomas Nelson (Hong Kong) Ltd
Toppan Building 10/F
22A Westlands Road
Quarry Bay Hong Kong

Thomas Nelson Australia
102 Dodds Street
South Melbourne
Vic 3205 Australia

Nelson Canada
1120 Birchmount Road
Scarborough Ontario
M1K 5G4 Canada

© Ken Blackford and John Humphries 1980

First published by E. J. Arnold and Son Ltd
ISBN 0-560-03498-9

This edition published by Thomas Nelson and Sons Ltd 1991
ISBN 0-17-410308-5
NPN 9 8 7 6 5 4 3 2

All rights reserved. No paragraph of this publication may be reproduced, copied or transmitted save with written permission or in accordance with the provisions of the Copyright, Design and Patents Act 1988, or under the terms of any licence permitting limited copying issued by the Copyright Licensing Agency, 90 Tottenham Court Road, London W1P 9HE.

Any person who does any unauthorised act in relation to this publication may be liable to criminal prosecution and civil claims for damages.

Printed in Great Britain by Bell and Bain Ltd, Glasgow

Introduction

It is a fact of school life that every teacher is, at some time or other, asked to take over an unfamiliar class or age group at a moment's notice. Many teachers can step into such a situation and produce a lesson, organise an activity or promote a discussion which is both enjoyable and educationally valuable; for the less experienced, covering for a colleague can be a difficult, even daunting task, while even experienced teachers may be asked to fill in so often that the imaginative well finally runs dry. It is hoped that every primary and middle school teacher will find this collection of quickly organised lessons useful, enjoyable and educationally worthwhile.

Each lesson is 'self-contained' and need not be followed up (though it should be pointed out that most can be extended if required). The lessons do not tamper with any syllabus or sequence or attempt to fit in with specific schemes of work (they may however be used to introduce or supplement many of the topics which would be covered in the normal course of events). The requirements for equipment and lesson preparation are minimal.

The layout of each lesson has been planned so that, at a glance, the teacher will have an idea of the approximate length of time required, though the lessons are flexible enough to fill whatever time is available; he will have a guide as to the age range covered by each activity and be able to note the aim and nature of each lesson together with whatever materials, preparation and organisation are needed. It is hoped that this format will allow him to decide very quickly how he may best use or adapt the lesson to suit his own purposes. A table of contents sub-divides the lessons for easy reference.

A certain amount of background information has been included for the teacher's use; this is by no means exhaustive, but should be sufficient to introduce the lesson and to use in class discussion. A specific activity, however, rather than a lot of talking is the central feature of each lesson. Suggestions for further activities have been included where relevant.

The lessons range from English to Number and from P.E. to Art. Many are already firm favourites, tried and tested over the years, some are variations of these, while others are new. It is hoped that in making them all available in a single volume they will be a source of inspiration and will prove useful to the experienced and the inexperienced alike, so that whenever the need arises to take a class at short notice, the ensuing activity will be an enjoyable and valuable experience for both children and teacher.

Contents

	page
Introduction	7
Art and Design	
All-edible plants	10
Calligrams	12
Dot pictures	14
Postage stamp design	16
Shadow pictures	18
Codes and Communication	
Porta's box and dot cipher	20
Non-verbal communication	22
Space messages	24
English Language	
Alphabet based activities	
Alphabetic sentences	26
Holo-alphabetic sentences	28
Poetry puzzle	30
The most popular letter	32
Oral work	
Situations	34
Spelling and Vocabulary	
Crosspoints	36
Linked words	38
Palindromes	40
Two-letter words	42
Word chains	44
Word squares	46
Geography	
Map colouring	48
Registration letters	50
Mathematics	
Area	
Make the man grow	52
Co-ordinates	
Bird in a square	54
Four rules	
Ancient Egyptian multiplication	56
Lattice multiplication	58
Magic squares	60
Napier's Bones	62
Nomograms	64

Number combination square	66
Number sequences	
Intersecting lines	68
Ones and twos	70
Permutations	
What makes a good pupil?	72
Probability	
The Derby	74
Shape	
Curves of pursuit	76
Networks	78
Polyominoes	80
Pentomino puzzle	82
Tangrams	84
Symmetry	
Mirror reflections	86

Physical Activities
Ball games	
Anyball	88
Chairball	90
Hand hockey	92
Non-stop cricket	94
Drama	
The burglary	96

Reasoning, Logic
When?	100
Filling a zoo	102
Flow diagram — *investigating diff methods of presenting info.*	104
Survival	106
Tower of Hanoi	108

Science
Eyes	110
Fingerprints	112
Paper aeroplanes	114
Reactions	116

Solutions, further information
Magic Square solution	118
Pentominoes solution	119
Tangram solution	120

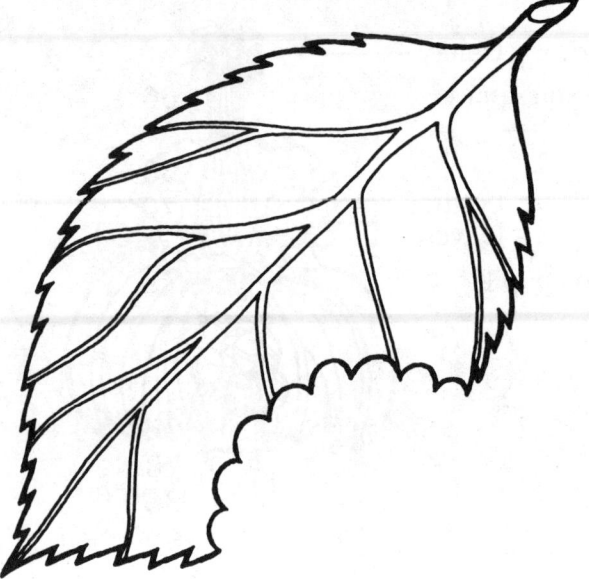

ALL-EDIBLE PLANTS

Background information
[To be used when planning the lesson]
Edible parts of a plant

Roots – beetroot, carrot, parsnip, radish, sugarbeet, tapioca.

Stems – asparagus, bamboo shoots, leeks, sugar cane, potatoes (tuber), onions (bulb), rhubarb (N.B. A tuber is a swollen underground stem. A bulb is both stem and leaves).

Leaves – lettuce, parsley, spinach, tea, watercress.

Leaf stalks – rhubarb, celery.

Flower buds – cabbage, Brussels sprouts.

Flowers – cauliflower, sprouting broccoli.

Seeds – cocoa beans (in pod), coffee bean, walnut, pea, broad bean.

Fruits – apple, banana, corn on the cob, cucumber, marrow, orange, runner bean, strawberries, tomatoes, etc., etc.

Preparation
Write the following headings across the blackboard: *Roots Stems Leaves Leaf-stalks Flower-buds Flowers Seeds Fruits*

Discussion
Talk about foods, the children's favourite foods, and foods which are plants or made from plants.

Discuss which parts of a plant are edible. Ask the children to name the parts of the plants which we eat and to give examples. Write the examples under the correct headings on the blackboard.

Time required
30 minutes

Age range
7–11 years

Aim
To provide a stimulus for imaginative thinking and drawing.

Organisation
Children will work individually.

Equipment
Each child will need
    paper and pencil
    crayons or felt tipped pens

Activity
Ask the children to draw a plant using as many different edible parts as possible.

Dependent on the children's confidence to use their own imagination on this project the teacher will use the picture example before, during or after the individual drawings have been started.

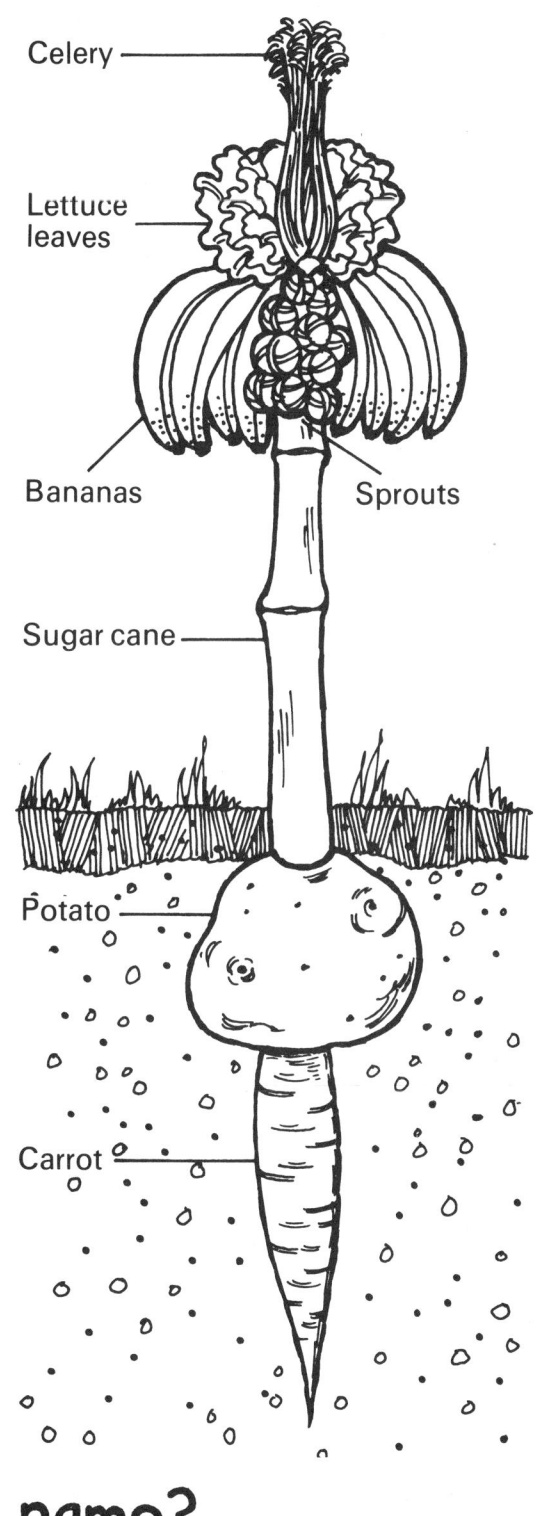

name?

11

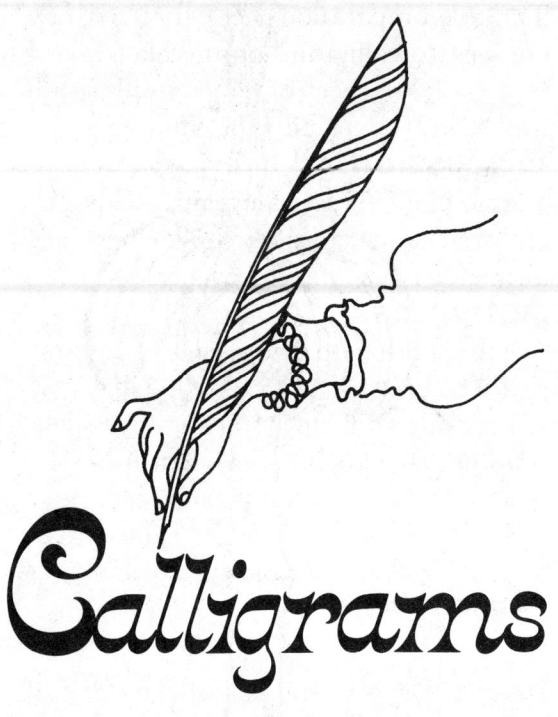

Calligrams

LOOK

SANDWICH (mirrored below)

AWAY

BEND

DOTS (in dots)

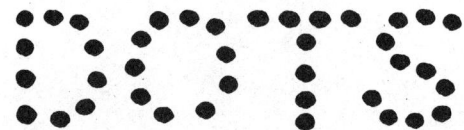

Time required
10–30 minutes
Age range
10–13 years
Aim
To have fun with words.
Organisation
Children will usually work individually, but may work in pairs.
Equipment
Each child will need
    paper and pencil
    crayons, if available
Background information
A calligram is a design using the letters of a word. It may be appropriate to mention that the word calligraphy is derived from the Greek words, *kallos* – beauty and *graphein* – to write.
The following are examples:

Preparation
The only preparation necessary is to draw one or two calligrams on the blackboard or on a large sheet of paper to illustrate what you are expecting the children to do.

Discussion
Talk about these calligrams with the children and consider how they are formed. Discuss the effectiveness of each.

Activities
Ask the children to devise some calligrams of their own.

If they have difficulty starting give them some of the following words first:

worms	shiver	lift	stretch
fire	tears	stripes	catapult
break	plants	balloons	football
bump	clock	stool	measles

Children could design posters or advertisements using calligrams.

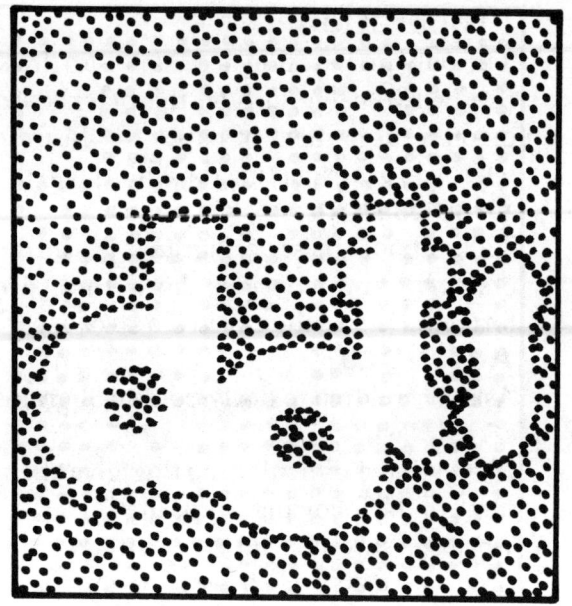

Background information
Printed pictures are made up of dots. Generally, the density of colour or the darkness of the shades is determined by the size of the dots. In monochrome pictures, the lighter the picture the larger the dots; this ensures that many variations of shade can be obtained. These effects are easily seen in newspaper pictures.

Preparation
If possible the children should be given a newspaper or a newspaper picture. Using a felt tipped pen on a large sheet of white paper the teacher may wish to show the class how to obtain different effects by varying the size, density and position of the black dots.

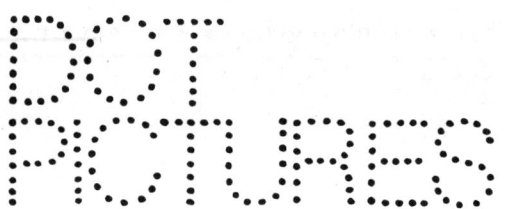

Discussion
Tell the children that drawing pictures using dots is quite difficult but that drawing patterns first is a good way to start. Talk about the different results possible using the dot technique:
- scattered dots or points of equal size (fig. 1)
- loose rows (fig. 2)
- dispersion, lines and figures using dots of varying shape and size (fig. 3)

Time required
20 minutes
Age range
9–13 years
Aim
To experiment with picture composition.
Organisation
Children should work on their own.
Equipment
Each child will need
- a felt tipped pen (but a pencil or crayon will do)
- a piece of paper
- a few newspaper pictures

Activity
To devise a pattern or design using a dot technique.

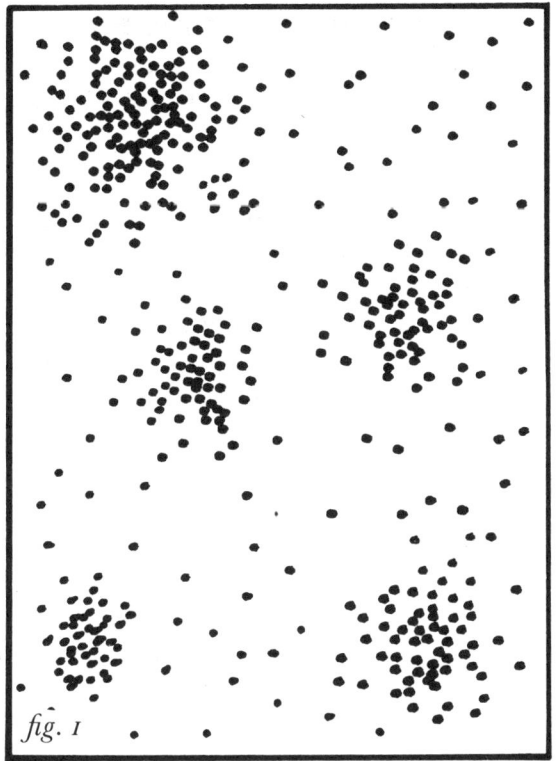
fig. 1

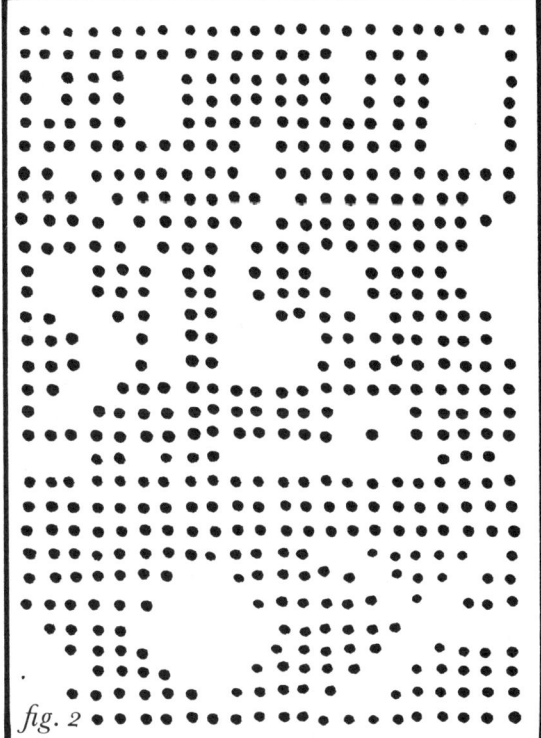
fig. 2

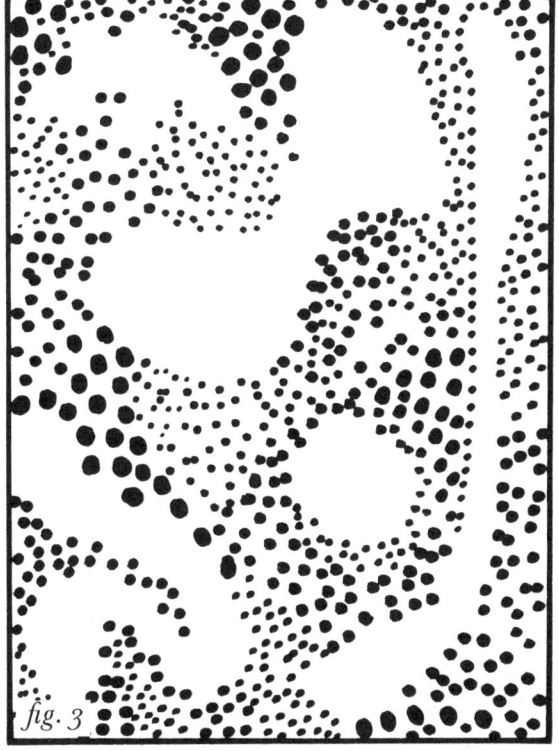
fig. 3

Further activities
1 The quality of the designs will improve as children realise the possibilities of the technique and become skilled at spreading the dots and forming shapes.
2 Children could be asked to draw a picture using the dot method.
3 Children could experiment with colour, especially colour mixing to produce different hues ... a mixture of red and blue dots for instance will produce a purple effect.

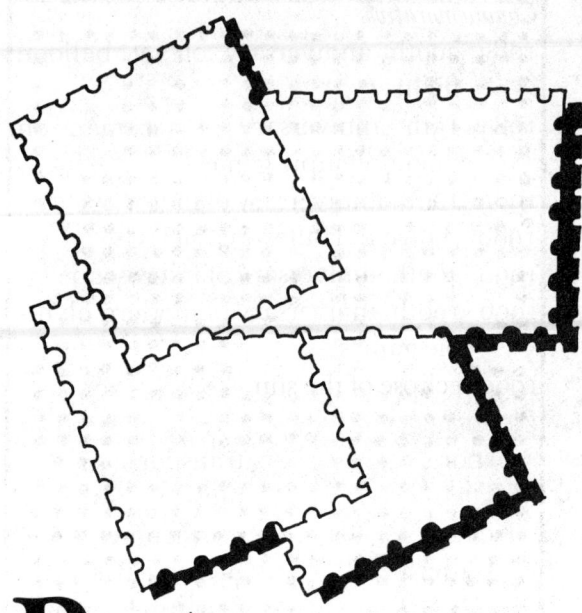

Postage Stamp Design

Time required
30 minutes

Age range
9–13 years

Aim
To introduce an art form within strict design limitations.

Organisation
Children should work individually but may sit in groups to use paints or crayons.

Equipment
Each child will need
- a piece of white drawing paper
- a pencil
- ruler
- pencils, crayons, felt pens or paints

Background information
Postage stamps came into use for the first time, anywhere in the world, in Britain on 6 May, 1840. Until that time the postal system was very expensive and it was the recipient rather than the sender of a letter who paid for the service. In 1840, letters with postage stamps could be sent anywhere in Britain for one penny per half ounce in weight. Two stamps were produced originally (without perforations) in sheets of 240 – the penny black and the twopenny blue. The penny black was only used for one year before being replaced by the penny red. There were no perforated stamps until 1854.

Definitive stamps are the standard stamps always available and British definitives are usually small, bearing the monarch's head, the value and very little else; they do not even have to bear the name of the country as they do everywhere else in the world. Special stamps called commemorative stamps or pictorials are now issued quite regularly – the first one in Britain was for the British Empire Exhibition in 1924.

Preparation
The teacher may like to draw a stamp 'shape' on the blackboard. Most commemorative stamps now measure 41 mm × 24 mm, but the artist's designs have to be four times bigger – 164 mm × 96 mm. The children may use this size or may work on a larger scale. It may be helpful if the teacher can draw a rough outline shape of The Queen's head on the blackboard, pointing out that this must appear somewhere on the stamp.

Commemorative

- 1983 200th anniversary of 1st balloon flight
- 1984 15th anniversary of 1st man on moon/olympic games
- 1985 100th anniversary of motor cycle
- 1986 return of Halley's comet
- 1990 400th anniversary of microscope
- 1996 100th anniversary of modern olympic games
- 1999 eclipse of the sun

Pictorial

sport	transport
keep-fit	musical
dogs	instruments
butterflies	British cities
flowers	Christmas

Further activities

1. Design a set of stamps on a single theme.
2. The lesson can be used as an introduction to the design of posters and advertisements.
3. First day cover stamps and special issues can be examined and discussed.

Activity

To design a pictorial or commemorative stamp. The teacher may suggest an event or let the children decide on one for themselves. The following lists may be of use in the discussion.

SHADOW PICTURES

Preparation
Each child will need to look through a newspaper until he finds a picture of someone's face, preferably at least 10 cm × 8 cm. Alternatively, the teacher could collect pictures beforehand and distribute a picture to each child at the beginning of the lesson. The picture must show a fair amount of shadow on the face (at least one third). In order not to discourage non-artistic or diffident children it is a good idea to demonstrate each stage of the process, leaving the examples available for examination.

Time required
30–40 minutes

Age range
10–13 years

Aim
To experiment with a contemporary art form using the relationship between light and shadow.

Organisation
Children to work individually.

Equipment
    a pile of newspapers or a prepared set of newspaper portraits, at least 10 cm × 8 cm
    glue

Each child must have
    scissors
    tracing paper
    a piece of white paper
    a black felt pen or black wax crayon
    lead pencil

Activity

Cut out the picture leaving a square or rectangle around the face. Cover with tracing paper and trace round all the areas which are black or dark grey. Transfer outlines on to plain paper and colour in shaded areas, using black felt pen or crayon.

Further activities

Children could be encouraged to experiment further by:

1. cutting round the shapes and mounting them onto different coloured paper
2. placing strips of identical pictures together in blocks using different colours to form a larger picture
3. using shadow pictures in some form of design – as the background for a poster, for example,
4. trying the same methods with pictures of objects
5. drawing silhouettes using black paint or felt pen.

```
P │ O │ R
──┼───┼──
T │ A'│ S
──┼───┼──
B │ O │ X
```

PORTA'S BOX AND DOT CIPHER

Time required
30 minutes

Age range
7–11 years

Aim
To introduce children to coding systems.

Organisation
Children to work individually at first and later in pairs.

Equipment
Each child will need paper and pencil

Background information
This code was devised by an Italian, Giambattista della Porta in the 16th century.

Preparation
Write the following code on the blackboard.

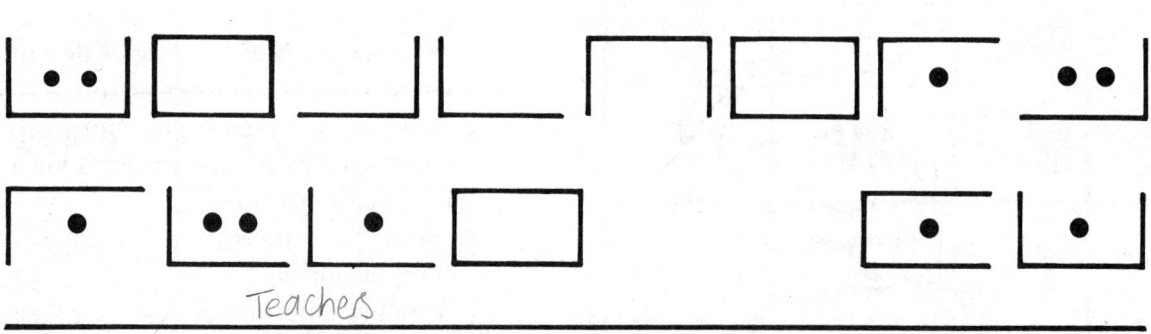

Teachers Rule O.K.

Discussion
Ask the children if they can decipher the code. Most codes they are likely to know are based on the alphabet and a number line.

Activity

Ask the children to write down the alphabet, then ask them to draw three 'noughts and crosses' boxes with the alphabet fitted into the squares as shown.

A	B	C
D	E	F
G	H	I
J	K	L
M	N	O
P	Q	R
S	T	U
V	W	X
Y	Z	

Ask if anyone can now decipher the code which is on the blackboard. If not substitute the letters for dots as shown.

The children will now be able to decipher the code and each child should write a coded message to his neighbour and decipher one in return.

Further activities

This lesson could introduce a topic on codes generally, during which children could invent their own codes, write stories which feature the use of codes and learn about the Morse Code and the semaphore system.

NON·VERBAL COMMUNICATION

Preparation
Draw the following on the blackboard.

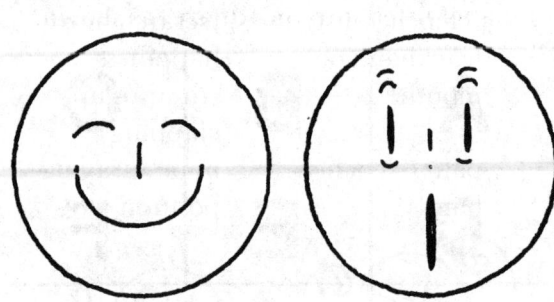

Time required
30 minutes
Age range
10–12 years
Aim
To demonstrate that communication can be achieved in a variety of ways.
Organisation
Children to work individually.
Equipment
Each child will need
paper and pencil

Discussion
Ask the children which face says:
    I am angry
    I am concentrating
    I am afraid
    I am happy
    I am in pain
    It wasn't me

Ask the children to demonstrate with their hands the following communications (possible ways in brackets).

anger (clenched fist)
fear (hand on mouth)
pain (clenched hands)
concentration (scratch head)
happiness (thumbs up, clapping)
hope (praying position)

Ask the children to tell you how their hands communicate other emotions.

arguing (pointing)
explaining (palms spread)
refusing (hand held up).

Activity 1
Ask the children to draw stick men to show the following

I'm fed up.	*(hands on hips, foot tapping)*
I'm frightened!	*(knees knocking)*
I'm relaxed.	*(lying down, legs crossed)*
I'm ready to race.	*(leaning forward)*
I'm not moving!	*(legs, feet apart)*
I've won the football pools.	*(leaping about)*

Activity 2
Draw two profiles on the blackboard, one happy, the other unhappy.

Ask the children to draw a profile communicating:

What a nice smell!
What a horrible smell!
Do you want a fight?
Help! We're sinking.

Background information

Because of language difficulties involved in communicating with civilisations from outer space a 'mathematical message' needs to be used. These messages are based on dots and dashes sent by radio signals from radio telescopes. The easiest 'message' and one which another civilisation might assume we would send is a picture of ourselves. Bursts of 323 dots and dashes are transmitted. A civilisation capable of receiving such signals should realise that this number is divisible by only 17 and 19 and thus arrange the dots and dashes in rows of 17 and 19. When arranged in 19 rows of 17, the following picture of a man would be formed by filling in the dashes, starting in the top left-hand corner.

Space Messages

Time required
40 minutes

Age range
10–13 years

Aim
To demonstrate the use of mathematics in communication.

Organisation
Children should work in pairs.

Equipment
Each child will need
- a piece of large-squared paper (at least 7 squares × 9 squares)
- a pencil
- a strip of paper which is divided or divisible into at least 63 squares (may be joined together)

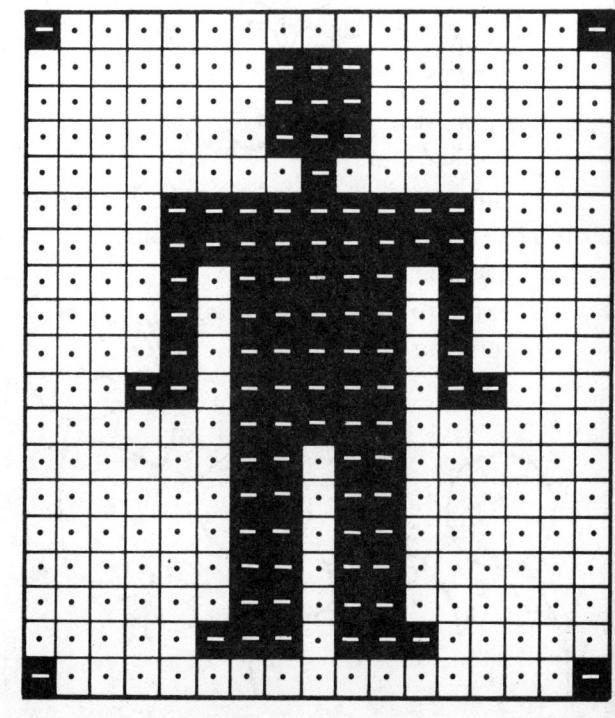

Preparation

This exercise can be done with a 7 × 9 rectangle and the teacher may like to demonstrate this on the blackboard. If so, the teacher should draw a rectangle which is divided up into 9 rows of 7 squares and then write out the following strip of 63 dots and dashes which represent a basic 'man'.

—·..........——.——..·——.——··...——
———...··——.——..·...——·——..——···
..·—

Discussion

Explain to the children the form in which messages to outer space are sent and then demonstrate by filling in the rectangle. Start by putting the first dash into the top left-hand square and then continuing along the top row so that the second dash goes into the top right-hand square. The sixth dot then goes into the first square on the left-hand side of the second row and so on until the last dash goes into the final square on the bottom right-hand corner. The message looks more effective if the squares marked with a dash are shaded.

Activity

Let the children imagine that they have received this 'message' from the planet Earth on some distant planet where they live. Using a rectangle of the same size ask the children to send a reply. (It would probably be a picture of what they look like and they may not have developed in the same way on their own planet.)

Further information and activities

1. Try and work out the strip of dots and dashes used to make up the man on the 17 × 19 rectangle.
2. Imagine that contact has been made both ways; what would be the next message?
3. Send a message to a partner and see if he can translate it.
4. To send a message to a planet travelling around earth's nearest star (Proxima Centauri) would take 4.3 years. To send a message to Beta Cygni, the nearest star believed to have a planet in orbit would take over 10 years. The reply would take another 10 years to get back to earth!

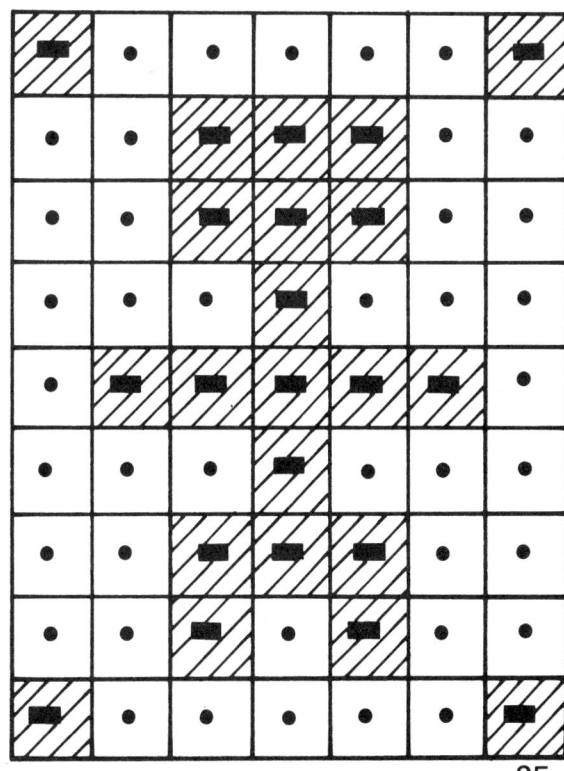

25

abcdef
ALPHABETIC SENTENCES

Time required
20 minutes
Age range
9–12 years
Aim
To make use of the alphabet sequence in sentence construction.
Organisation
Children can work individually or in pairs.
Equipment
Each child will need
  paper and pencil
  a dictionary (useful but not essential)

Background information
The idea of this lesson is to get the children to write a sentence or sentences with each successive word beginning with the next letter of the alphabet: *All Bad Children Deserve E F* etc.

Preparation

The teacher may like to write an 'alphabetic sentence' on the board – either one of his own or the following:

Animals Being Careful During Easter Find Good Homes In Jersey; Kind, Loving Masters, Near Open Pastures Quite Richly Situated, There, Under Vigilance, Will X-ray Your Zebra.

Discussion

It will probably be necessary to discuss the possibilities for the letters which may give most difficulty – J, Q, X, and Z.

J, Q, and Z are not too bad, but X is very restrictive, the best alternatives being:

    X-ray
    Xebec (a small three-masted vessel)
    Xenium (a present made to a guest, a ruler, or the church)
    Xylophone
    Xavier (a name)

Some teachers may be generous and allow Xmas.

Activity

To devise an alphabetic sentence. Providing a sequence is followed from the first letter it may be less daunting to begin with short sentences before attempting a full twenty-six word marathon. The teacher may allow some leeway by allowing the letters X and Z to appear anywhere in the word, instead of strictly at the beginning.

**ABCDEF
GHIJKL
MNOPQ
RSTUV
WXYZ**

Time required
20 minutes
Age range
10–13 years
Aim
To have fun with words and form a sentence which contains every letter of the alphabet.
Organisation
The children should work individually.
Equipment
Each child will need
  paper and pencil
  dictionary (useful but not essential)

HOLO-ALPHABETIC SENTENCES

Background information

A holo-alphabetic sentence is one which contains every letter of the alphabet and it may be worth pointing out that the word comes from the Greek word *holos* meaning whole. The most famous holo-alphabetic sentence is 'The quick brown fox jumps over the lazy dog'.

The *Guinness Book of Records* does not include a true holo-alphabetic sentence but it does quote two contrived newspaper headlines which contain all 26 letters once and only once. One of these reads – CWM FJORD-BANK GLYPHS VEXT QUIZ (describing the annoyance of an eccentric in finding inscriptions on the side of a fjord in a rounded valley). This is a bizarre example however and is not likely to be very helpful to the children.

Discussion

Write the 'quick brown fox' sentence on the board and ask the children what is special about it. Tell the class what a holo-alphabetic sentence is, and devise one jointly, writing it on the blackboard. It may be helpful to write out the alphabet for the children to refer to while the sentence is being created.

Activity

Each child should devise and write down the shortest possible holo-alphabetic sentence. The initial objective should be to beat a 50 letter limit. A sentence using less than 40 letters is quite difficult but it may be achieved by some of the more able children, or with the teacher's help.

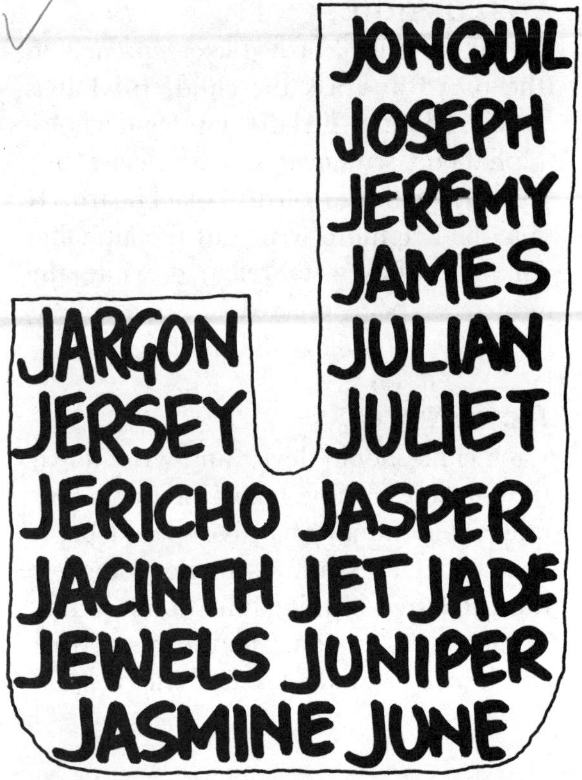

Background information

Jargon

Jerusalem, Joppa, Jericho –
These are the cities of long ago.

Jasper, jacinth, jet and jade –
Of such are jewels for ladies made.

Juniper's green and jasmine's white,
Sweet jonquil is spring's delight.

Joseph, Jeremy, Jennifer, James,
Julian, Juliet – just names.

January, July and June –
Birthday late or birthday soon.

Jacket, jersey, jerkin, jeans –
What's the wear for sweet sixteens?

Jaguar, jackal, jumbo, jay –
Came to dinner but couldn't stay.

Jellies, junkets, jumbals, jam –
Mix them up for sweet-toothed Sam.

To jig, to jaunt, to jostle, to jest –
These are the things that Jack loves best.

Jazz, jamboree, jubilee, joke –
The jolliest words you ever spoke.

From A to Z and Z to A
The joyfullest letter of all is J.

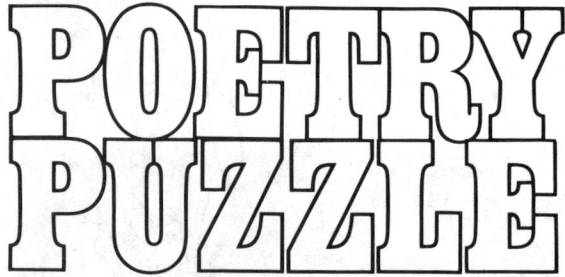

POETRY PUZZLE

Time required
40 minutes
Age range
10–12 years
Aim
To have fun with words.
Organisation
Children can work on their own or with a partner.
Equipment
Each child will need paper and pencil

Preparation
Read to the children the poem 'Jargon' which was written by James Reeves.
   Possibly write four or five verses on the blackboard so that they can see the form of the poem.

Discussion

Ask the children what they notice about the poem, *ie* the grouping of things in each verse beginning with the same letter of the alphabet. Choose another letter and show the children how to group items using that letter.

The letter A is used here as an example:

Names	*Gems*
Alice	agate
Angus	amber
Anthony	amazonite
Abraham	amethyst
Adam	aquamarine

Animals	*Countries*
antelope	Australia
ant	Argentina
adder	Austria
alligator	Afghanistan
albatross	Angola

Cities	*Trees*
Aberdeen	acacia
Athens	ash
Amsterdam	alder
Adelaide	apple
Auckland	aspen

Plants	*Continents*
alfalfa	Asia
aster	Africa
amaryllis	Australasia
anemone	Antarctica
azalea	America

Activity

Ask the children to choose a letter of their own, to write down some groups of items, and then to write their own poem.

Further activities

Possible discussion about alliteration with children. Children could then go on to write their own sentences using alliteration. *eg* The fearful fox fought five ferocious ferrets.

eeeeeeeeeee
ttttttttttt
aaaaaaaa
iiiiiiiii
sssssss
oooooo
nnnnn
hhhh
rrr
dd
u

The most popular letter

Time required
30 minutes
Age range
8–11 years
Aim
To discover the most commonly used letters in the English language – an exercise in tallying.
Organisation
Children can work individually or in pairs.
Equipment
Each child will need
    a book, comic or magazine
    paper and pencil

Background information
The most commonly used letters in the English language in order are:

etaisonhrdu

Preparation
On the blackboard you will need to write down a list of the letters of the alphabet in two or three columns, leaving sufficient space to write a number by the side of each letter.

Discussion

Tell the children that they are going to try to find out which is the most used letter in the English language. Ask them which they think is the most popular letter. They could write down the three which they think are the most commonly used.

Activities

Ask the children to start at the beginning of a page of a story or an article and to count 100 letters, then to put a tiny pencil mark above the 100th letter. They must then write down the letters of the alphabet in two columns:

a   n
b   o
c   p
d   q
e   r
f   s
g   t
h   u
i   v
j   w
k   x
l   y
m   z

Now ask the children to start at the beginning of their passage and, working on the first hundred letters, put a tally mark by the side of each letter on their lists as it occurs.

eg

a |||
b |
c
d ||
e |||| ||

Discussion

When this has been done ask each child how many tally marks he has beside each letter. Add all the results together and enter this number beside the letters on the blackboard. This will show the overall results very clearly and it will be obvious that they closely resemble the list printed under **background information**.

Further information and activities

The children can make graphs of their own results or the result of the group they are sitting in, and a graph to show the total class result.

The most popular initial letter is *t*, and the most popular written words in the English language in order are:
the, of, and, to, a, in, that, is, I, it.
The word most used in conversation is *I*.

As a further extension, children can be asked to try and write a story without using any word containing the letter *e*.

SITUATIONS

Time required
25 minutes

Age range
7–11 years

Aim
To encourage thoughtful conversation.

Organisation
Children should work in pairs. This lesson is suitable for either hall or classroom.

Equipment
Each child will need
    a chair

Background information
The idea of this lesson is to put children into one-to-one situations with each other and to encourage them to converse with a partner, imagining a particular situation. Three situations have been suggested for the activities – many others could be used. Each situation should be acted out twice so that each partner has a chance to 'play' both roles.

Preparation
Explain to the class that each situation must be thought about carefully before the conversations begin so that each part is played fluently and with conviction. Once the children have begun talking they should continue until they run out of things to say.

It may be necessary, if the children are not used to drama or speech work, to talk to them about each situation before they begin the activity.

Activities

The Dentist (One chair for patient)

The patient should be pleasant and should sit down and start a conversation with the dentist. The dentist should be as unpleasant as possible. He should be encouraged to be rough and to say and do things designed to frighten the patient.

This scene is 'designed' to help children act out their fears and the teacher should talk to the class about this when the children have played both parts. The scene could then be played out again with a kind, gentle dentist, to provide a useful contrast to the first situation.

The Interview
(A chair for each child – facing each other with desk or table between if available)

The interviewer should interview his partner for a job, preferably something requiring unusual qualifications – perhaps a spy, or a 'hand-made corkscrew twister'.

Short change
(Chairs or a table between each couple)

This should be an argument between the customer who believes he has paid with a five-pound note and the shopkeeper who believes it was a pound note. (This may get noisy although the shopkeeper should be encouraged to be as calm and firm as possible.)

Further activities

The children can develop role playing to a high level of sophistication which can result in exciting drama activities, both on a class level and in terms of more public performances – in particular school assemblies.

See also **The Burglary**, *page 96*.

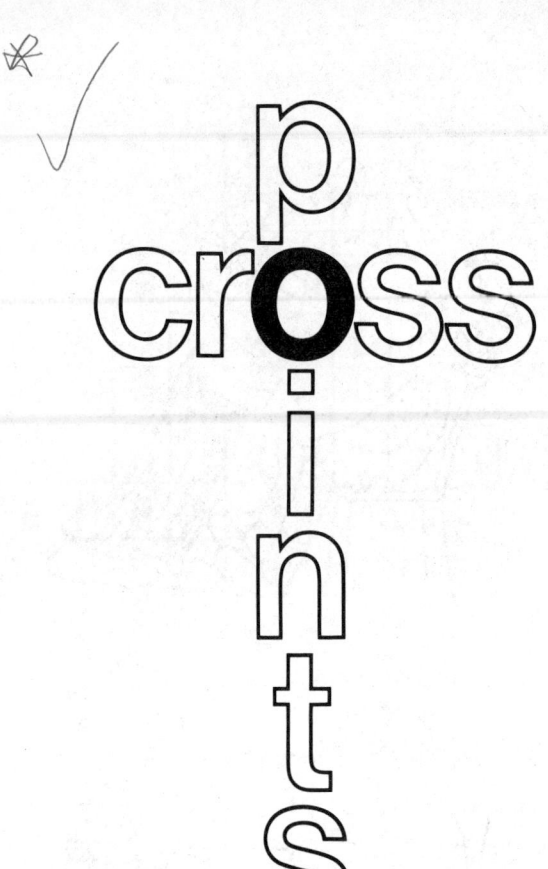

cross points

Background information
This lesson takes the form of a competitive word game using a grid similar to the one below.

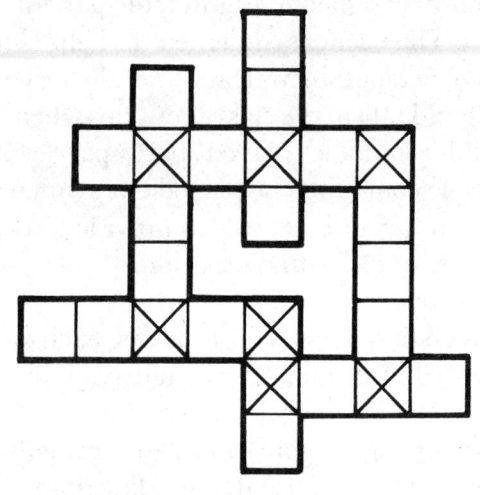

Time required
30 minutes

Age range
10–13 years

Aim
To reinforce spelling skills.

Organisation
Children should work individually, though it may be a good idea to let poor spellers work together.

Equipment
Each child will need
paper and pencil
dictionary if available

Children must fill in the grid with words of their own choice and gain points for the use of certain letters. A letter which falls on a 'cross' square is counted twice (once in the 'across' word and once in the 'down' word).

Preparation
Using the blackboard, draw a grid similar to the one above, and ask the children to copy it on to their paper. (This grid can be simplified or made more complex depending on the ability of the children.) While the children are doing this write down a list of the letters and their scores. Again these scores can be varied at will.

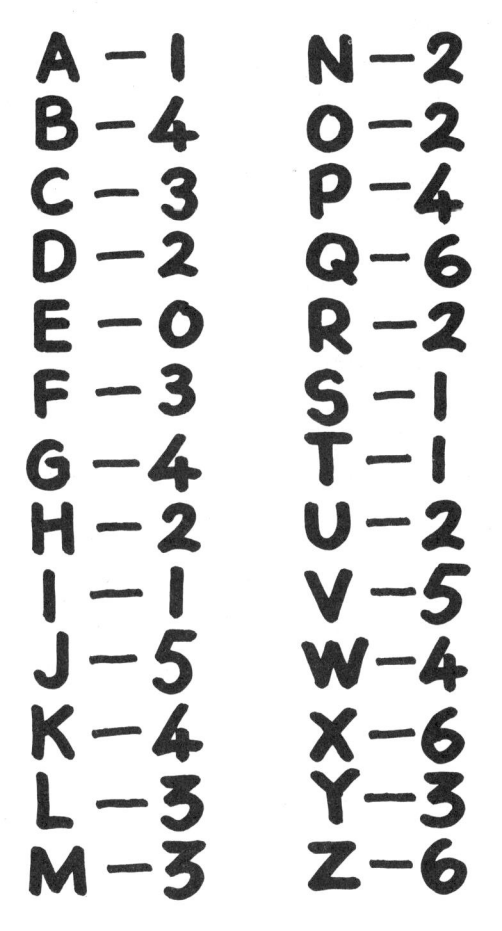

```
A - 1      N - 2
B - 4      O - 2
C - 3      P - 4
D - 2      Q - 6
E - 0      R - 2
F - 3      S - 1
G - 4      T - 1
H - 2      U - 2
I - 1      V - 5
J - 5      W - 4
K - 4      X - 6
L - 3      Y - 3
M - 3      Z - 6
```

```
           10
            P
        J   L
        A   A
    GARAGE   12
        U   L
        N   D
  7 LATER   E
      11  E A R N 5
          D     7
          4
```

points scored 56

Discussion
Explain to the children that they are to fill in the grid trying to score as many points as possible, and that they must of course spell correctly all the words they use. Demonstrate how letters in the 'cross' boxes score down and across.

Activity
Let the children fill in their grids, using dictionaries as necessary, until they are happy that they have as many points as possible. Generally children can count up their own scores with a little guidance or help from the teacher and have them checked by another child (or the teacher).

Further information and activities
1 Scores can either be compared within the class or children can be encouraged to beat their own score.
2 Shape and size of the grid and letter scores can be varied by the teacher, or the children themselves.

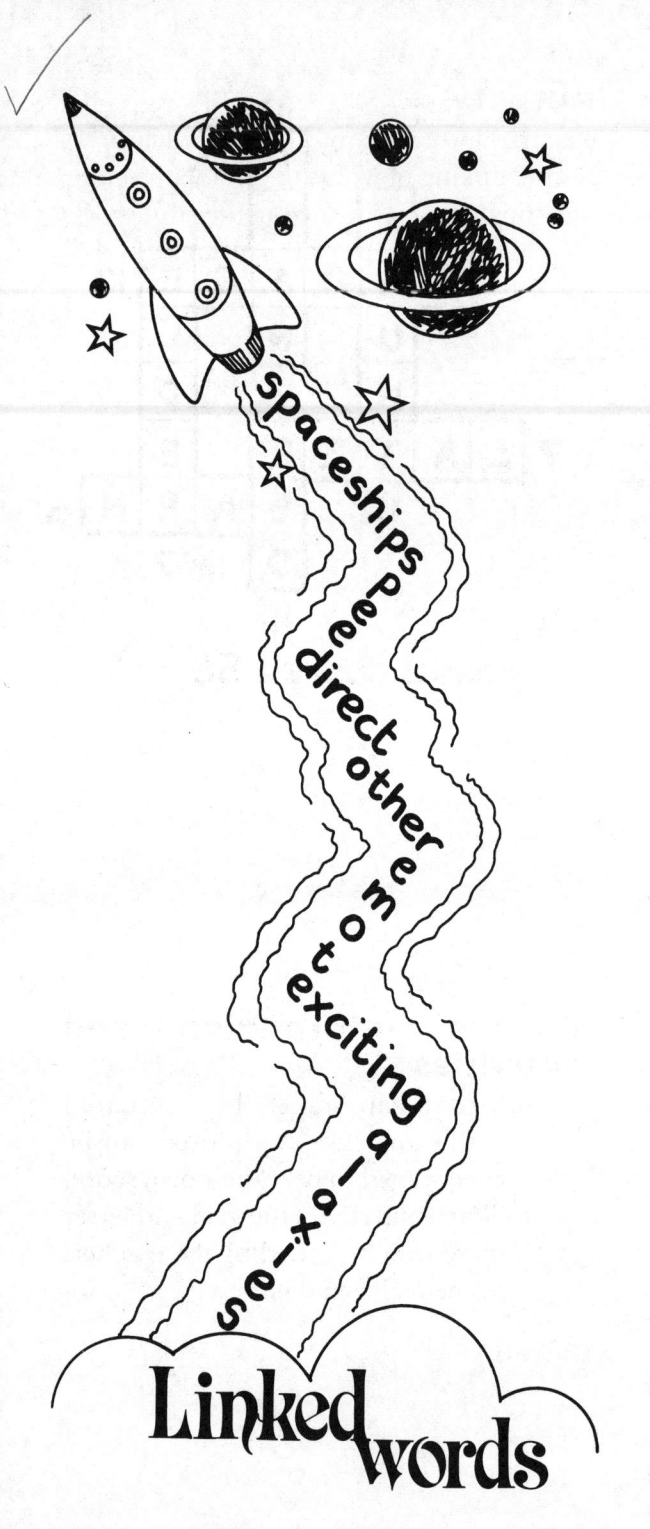

Time required
15 minutes

Age range
7–11 years

Aim
To promote spelling and vocabulary skills.

Organisation
Children should work individually.

Equipment
Each child will need
> paper and pencil
> dictionaries would be useful but are not essential

Background information
This is a lesson to encourage children to play with words. The idea is to get children to link words together by using the last letter of one word to become the first letter of the next word.

Linked words

spaceships exciting galaxies tomorrow other direct

sugar
rabbit
tomorrow
table
eating
ghost

The real skill of linked words, however, is not just to link the word, but also the meaning (Summer – roses – sunhat – travel – lovely – yellow – windbreak – kingcup – picnics – sandwich – hot .....) or to make them form a sentence or newspaper headline. (Spaceships speed direct to other remote exciting galaxies.)

Children also enjoy subject-linked chains. Animals are always a favourite.

Activity
To form a word ch
simple linking of w
meaning, dependi
the children and th

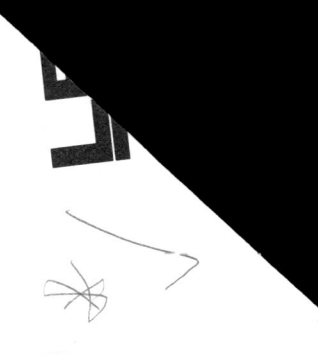

```
dog
 o
 a
 tiger
     e
     i
     n
     d
     e
     e
     rabbit
          o
          a
          dog
```

Ideally the chain should end with the same word as it started. It is also quite demanding to link words which have only a set number of letters (3, 4, 5 or 6):
their – rough – horse – every – yours – story – yacht – their

Background information

A palindrome is a word that reads the same backward as forwards. There are a large number of such words in the English language.

eg madam, pop, eve, did, dad, pip, noon, kayak, civic, redder, reviver, rotator, and, according to the *Guinness Book of Records*, the longest of all – REDIVIDER.

A palindromic sentence or paragraph is one that reads the same backwards as forwards (even though words may be split up differently) *eg* Madam, I'm Adam (reputedly the first words spoken by Adam to Eve) or Nurses run.

Palindromes

ABLE WAS I ERE I SAW ELBA

Time required
30 minutes
Age range
10–13 years
Aim
To have fun with words.
Organisation
Children should work individually or in pairs.
Equipment
Each child will need
  paper and pencil
  dictionaries would be useful but are not essential

Basically there are two ways of constructing a palindromic sentence. The first is simply to take words such as LIVE, SAW, RAT, and STEP (which all make new words when reversed) and put them together with a palindromic word in the middle; thus EVIL I LIVE or the very well known ABLE WAS I ERE I SAW ELBA, supposedly said by Napoleon but unfortunately not actually said by him! The more advanced stage is where one has to jump over gaps between words when reversing so as to make the palindromic sentence read truly – such as in MADAM I'M ADAM.

Other well known palindromes include
    WAS IT A RAT I SAW?
    DRAW, O COWARD.
    SUMS ARE NOT SET AS A TEST ON ERASMUS
and probably the greatest of all A MAN, A PLAN, A CANAL – PANAMA.

Discussion
Explain to the children what a palindrome is and how a sentence can be formed – probably only the simpler version first. Draw up two lists of words, one of true palindromic words (including I and A) and one of words which make another word when reversed.

Activity
To devise a palindromic sentence. In the first place it should not matter too much whether the sentence makes complete sense.

TWO-LETTER WORDS

Background information

This lesson is based on those words in the English language which consist of only two letters. The exact number of such words is debatable because they fall into several categories:

> common words
> exclamations and interjections
> childish words, foreign words, words in uncommon use, names of notes
> abbreviations

The teacher must decide for himself or herself which to allow. The most common ones in each category are as follows.

common words

am	by	in	no	so
an	do	is	of	to
as	go	it	on	up
at	he	me	or	us
be	if	my	ox	we

exclamations and interjections

Ah	Hi	Oh
Bo	Ho	Ta
Eh	La	Wo
Ha	Lo	

childish, foreign, unusual, musical notes

Ay (yes)	Mi (musical)	Ti or Te (musical)
Ex (no longer, from, out of)	Pa (father)	Ye
Id (fish, biological, psychological term)		Pi (mathematical)
Ma (mother)		Ti (tree)

abbreviations in common use

Ed – Editor   Al – Alan   Vi – Violet   Jo – Josephine

Time required
30 minutes

Age range
9–11 years

Aim
To practise spelling two-letter words.

Organisation
Class discussion followed by children working individually or in pairs.

Equipment
Each child will need
> paper and pencil
> dictionary (if available)

Preparation
The teacher may like to prepare lists of two-letter words, either on a blackboard, or a large piece of paper, hidden from view.

Discussion
Discuss with, and try to elicit from the children, as many two-letter words as possible. You may need to add to this list, but by going through the alphabet most classes should be able to come up with the twenty-five common words.

Activity
To write a little story using two-letter words only. This is not easy, but with a little help, and maybe an example, most children can arrive at what usually turns out to be an amusing paragraph. A conversation is the easiest to write and is often more effective if the children work in pairs to produce it. 'Reading out' from such a dialogue can provide a lot of enjoyment for the class.

> Is it Pa?
> It is!
> He is on it.
> Is he?
> He is, or my Ma is.
> No, Ma is on an ox.
> On an Ox?
> Ay.
> Lo! My Ma is on an ox!
> Is it Ma?
> Ay.
> Oh no!
> Ma, Ma, no.
> Wo! Wo!
> Oh no, Ma is in it!

Further activities
The children could try to write sentences using three or five-letter words only.

WORD CHAINS

Time required
15 minutes

Age range
9–11 years

Aim
To practise spelling and word construction.

Organisation
Children to work individually or in pairs.

Equipment
Each child will need
- paper and pencil
- dictionary (useful but not essential)

Background information
The idea of this lesson is to introduce the children to compound words and to encourage them to recognise words within words.

Discussion
Explain what compound words are and give some examples. Ask the children to think of compound words and to break them up into their constituent parts. It will be important to stress that the same spelling can be pronounced in more than one way. Discuss how a word chain can be made in which the final part of one word forms the beginning of the next word:

eg

horseman
mankind
kindred
redskin
skinflint
flintlock

Activity
To create the longest possible word chain.

Further information and activities
This idea can be used as a round for a class or group activity. One child starts the chain and each child in turn provides the next link in the chain. The teacher may need to give some words to start the children off. Here are some which may be useful:

enlist

railway

houseboat

This activity will lead quite naturally on to discussion of syllables and letter strings and thus on to further spelling games.

WORD SQUARES

Time required
10–30 minutes

Age range
8–11 years

Aim
To provide spelling practice while allowing children to 'play with words'.

Organisation
Children must work in pairs, sitting opposite each other.

Equipment
Each child will need
  paper and pencil
  a dictionary would be useful for checking words

Preparation
Children should draw a 5 cm square and then divide it into 1 cm squares. In order to explain the game clearly it would be best for the teacher to play a game against one of the children – the child with his back to the board and the teacher drawing his square on the blackboard so the rest of the class can see. Scoring is then easily demonstrated at the end of the game.

Method of play
Each player should keep his square hidden from his opponent. Turns are taken to call out a letter which both players must place somewhere in their respective squares. The object is to spell as many words as possible in the rows and columns. Names, abbreviations and foreign words are not allowed.

Here is an example game up to the first ten letters to show how two players can elect to use the letters called:

Player Calls

	1	2
1	K	
2		B
3	A	
4		R
5	Y	
6		E
7	A	
8		K
9	N	
10		E

Scoring

Points are scored on the following scale:

 5 letter word – 6 points
 4 letter word – 4 points
 3 letter word – 3 points
 2 letter word – 2 points

No one letter can be used to score in more than one word in any row or column, *eg* S O B E T. This can be scored as SO and BET, but not as SOB and BET.

Activities

Let the children play against each other in pairs. At the end of the game the children should check each other's squares together so that agreement is reached on the final scores.

Further activities

Children could make bigger squares producing longer words. Children could work alone to fill a 5 × 5 square with the object of making as high a score as possible. The most valuable exercise could be to ask the children to make up their own word games – encouraging the use of dictionaries. Such games would be tested by other children in the class.

Player 1

K	A	Y	A	K
	N		B	
	E		E	
	R			

Player 2

B	A	K	E	
R				
A	N			
K		Y		
E				

See also **Magic Squares,** *page* **60**. A completed word square reading the same down as across may be possible.

MAP COLOURING

Time required
30 minutes

Age range
9–12 years

Aim
To demonstrate that only four colours are needed to colour any geographical map.

Organisation
Children should work individually.

Equipment
Ideally the teacher should have a wall map or atlas for demonstration purposes but this is not essential.
Each child will need
> paper and pencil
> coloured pencils (which may be shared)

Background information

When colouring a geographical map it is common practice to give different colours to any two countries (or counties) which have a common border. No map has yet been devised, no matter how many divisions on it, which needs more than four colours. This is assuming that areas which meet at a single point are not considered to have a common border – no confusion would arise if two such areas *were* the same colour.

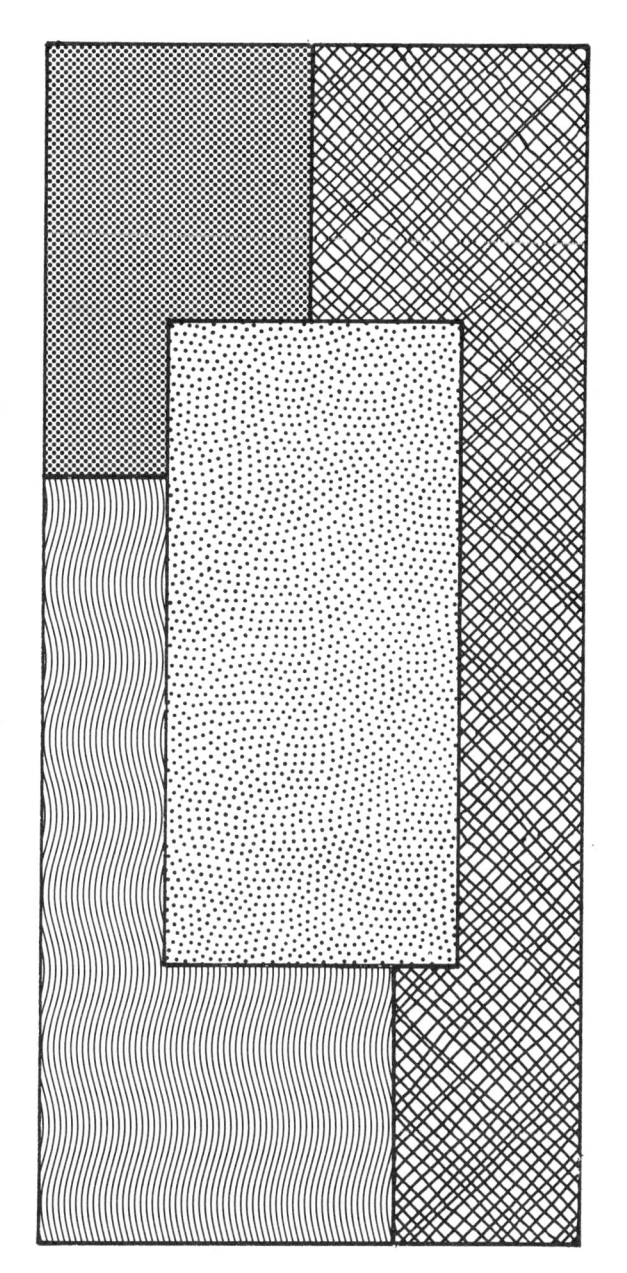

Discussion

Talk with the children about maps of countries and how they are coloured so that each country can be seen clearly. Show the class a wall map or have an atlas available. (Most atlases in fact use more than four colours though this is not strictly necessary.)

Activity

To draw an island continent of their own 'design' with as many different countries as they like, situated in any way they like. The children should then colour these maps, using only four colours. (The teacher can safely offer a large reward for anyone who finds it necessary to use five colours.)

Further activities

May be used as an introduction to map work.

This simple illustration shows a definite need for four different colours – because each country has a common border with the other three.

[Handwritten note: Use an intro to fishing transport or seat coastal cards!]

REGISTRATION LETTERS

Background information
Sea fishing boats have to be registered with HM Customs and Excise. Boats carry letters followed by a number and these letters identify the port of registration. Often the letters are the first and last letters of the port concerned, but not always.

The original Licensing Authority of British cars is revealed by the last two letters. Registration GDU 142 A shows that the vehicle was registered in Coventry (DU = Coventry). The letters after the number show the year – in this case 1963 (A = 1963).

Preparation
Tell the children you are going to talk about registration letters. Ask them to think of examples of their use. Cars are the most obvious. Talk to the children about the uses of such letters: *eg* issue of licences, tracking down of stolen cars, identification of vehicles used in crimes.

Time required
30 minutes

Age range
7–11 years

Aim
To familiarise children with the fishing ports of the British Isles.

Organisation
The children should either work individually or in pairs, according to the preference of the teacher and the availability of atlases.

Equipment
Each child or pair of children will need
    an atlas
    paper and pencil

Discussion
Discuss local registration letters. Talk about the International Identity Marks seen on the back of vehicles showing from which countries they come. Ask the children if they can think of any. The most common are:

GB – Great Britain, B – Belgium, CH – Switzerland, D – West Germany, F – France, I – Italy, NL – Netherlands, IRL – Republic of Ireland.

Some less common ones which may be seen are:

A – Austria, CDN – Canada, DK – Denmark, E – Spain, GBG – Guernsey, GBJ – Jersey, GBM – Isle of Man, NZ – New Zealand, S – Sweden, ZA – South Africa.

Activity

Write the following fishing boat registration letters on the blackboard and ask the children to identify the ports of origin, using atlases if necessary. Point out that they may not all be the first and last letters, but that where they are not there is always a good reason, *eg* Penzance, Poole (PZ and PE). These are all British ports:

CF – Cardiff	CS – Cowes	DE – Dundee
DR – Dover	FD – Fleetwood	FE – Folkestone
GW – Glasgow	GY – Grimsby	HH – Harwich
LK – Lerwick	LL – Liverpool	LT – Lowestoft
PH – Plymouth	PZ – Penzance	OB – Oban
SA – Swansea	SH – Scarborough	SR – Stranraer
	PE – Poole	

Further information and activities

All civil aircraft must have registration marks. The first group of letters shows the country of origin, the second group identify the aircraft:

eg CCCP – AXY means aeroplane AXY from Russia.

Other useful aircraft registration letters are:

CF – Canada	D – W Germany	DDR – E Germany
EC – Spain	F – France	G – United Kingdom
HB – Switzerland	JA – Japan	N – United States
SU – Egypt	VH – Australia	VT – India

This lesson may be used as an introduction to topics on fishing, transport or the sea and coastal lands.

Preparation
Draw a 'square' man on the blackboard.

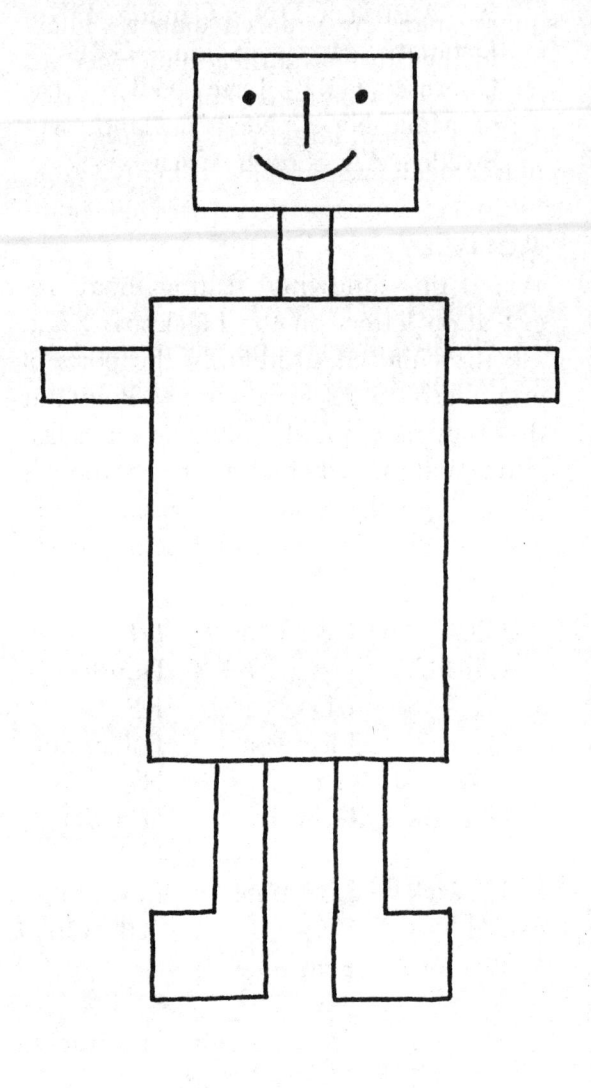

MAKE THE MAN GROW

Time required
30 minutes
Age range
8–10 years
Aim
To demonstrate the relationship between area and external dimensions.
Organisation
Children to work as a class and individually.
Equipment
Each child will need
      a piece of paper (small squares)
      a pencil

Activity 1
The children should draw their own square man on squared paper. They should then draw another man twice as tall. Care must be taken not to make the first figure too large thus making the enlargement impossible. Finally, the children can draw their original man twice as big.

Discussion
The children should appreciate that the man who is just twice as tall has changed shape, but the man who is twice as big is the same shape but considerably bigger. How much bigger?

Activity 2
All the children can draw a square head of the same size, say 2 × 2 squares.

The children can then draw the head twice the size by doubling the length of both sides. The children should notice that the area of the head is now four times bigger (2 × 2 = 4).

If the sides of the head are made three times longer then the area will increase (3 × 3) 9 times.

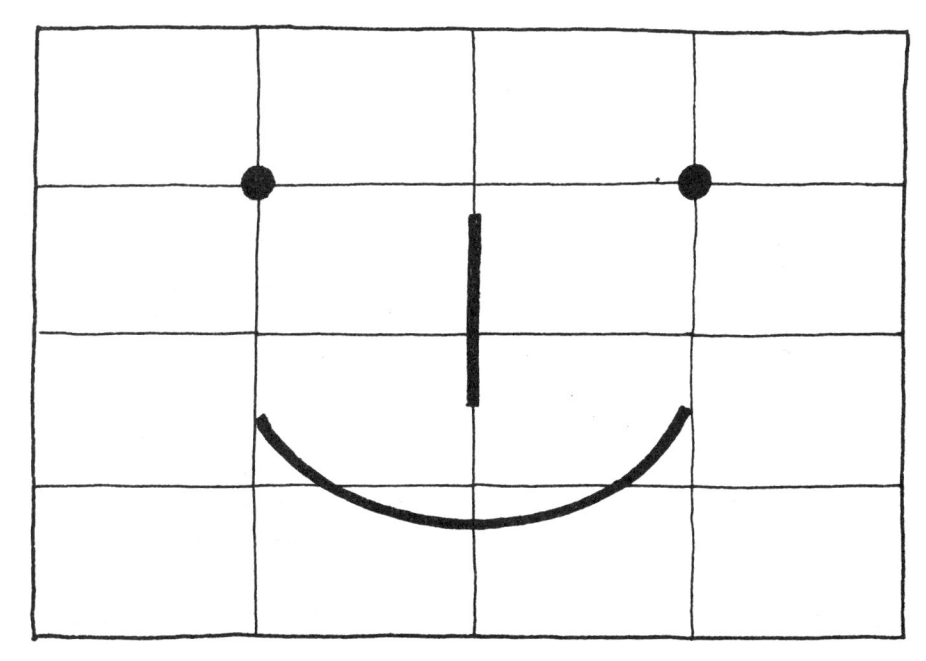

Bird in a square

Background information
When plotting a co-ordinate point the bottom (horizontal) number is always given first followed by the vertical number.

Preparation
Draw a ten by ten square on the blackboard. This will be necessary if the subject of co-ordinates is new to the class. Number as shown.

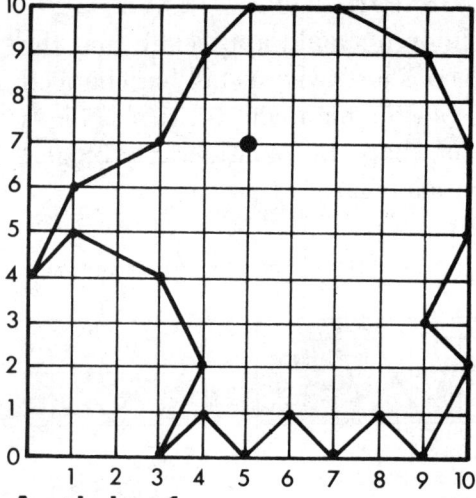

Activity 1
Ask the children to draw a 10 × 10 square on squared paper (there is no need to rule in all the small squares).

Read out the following co-ordinates for the children to mark on their squares with dots. After reading out the second co-ordinate join the two points, using a ruler. After reading out the third co-ordinate join that to the second. Continue until the drawing is complete. Demonstrate the process on the board.

(5,10) (4,9) (3,7) (1,6) (0,4) (1,5) (3,4) (4,2) (3,0) (4,1) (5,0) (6,1) (7,0) (8,1) (9,0) (10,2) (9,3) (10,5) (10,7) (9,9) (7,10) joined to (5,10). A large round dot can be made at 5,7 for the eye of this very simple bird's head.

Time required
40 minutes

Age range
9–11 years

Aim
To use co-ordinates in picture making

Organisation
Children will work as a class and in pairs.

Equipment
Each child will need
- a piece of squared paper
- a pencil
- a ruler

Activity 2

The children can now devise their own pictures using 10 × 10 squares and read out the co-ordinates for their partners to follow. It will soon become obvious to the children that a better picture is obtained if halves are introduced into the co-ordinate readings.

Further information and activities

If line drawings are too simple for a particular class or age group it would be advisable to omit the first part of this lesson and concentrate on using co-ordinates to identify various points on a map or plan or to plot a route through a series of obstacles marked on say, a 20 × 20 square grid.

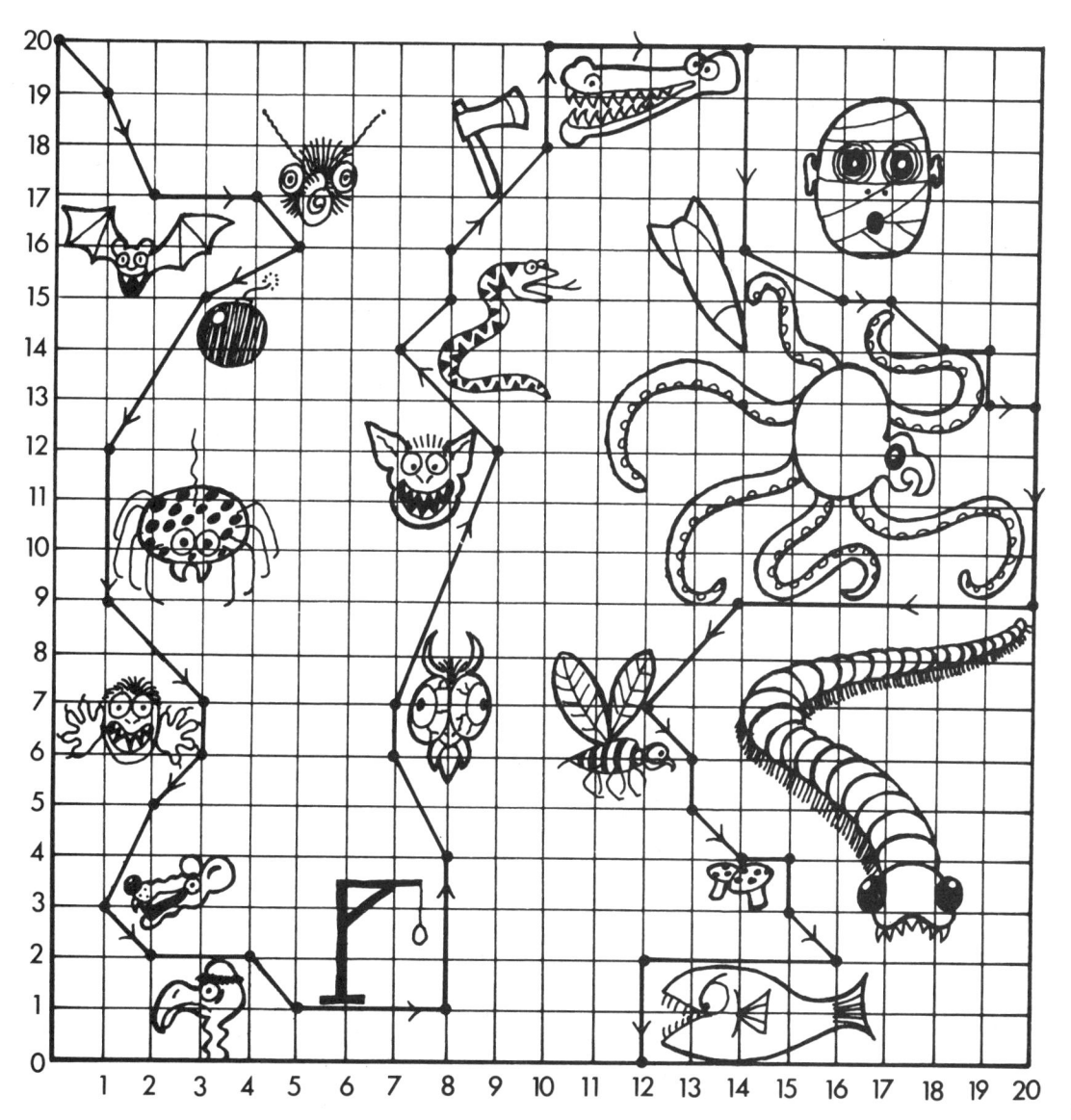

Background information
If the Ancient Egyptians wished to multiply 48 by 27 they used the following method.

example 1

$$48 \times 27$$
$$96 \times 13$$
$$\cancel{192 \times 6}$$
$$384 \times 3$$
$$768 \times 1$$
$$\overline{1296}$$

Ancient Egyptian multiplication

Time required
20 minutes

Age range 10–13 years

Aim
To introduce an alternative method of multiplication.

Organisation
Children can work individually or in pairs.

Equipment
Each child will need paper and pencil

Numbers in the left-hand column are doubled.
Numbers in the right-hand column are halved and any remainder is left out.
Whenever the numbers in the right-hand column are even, the row is crossed out.
To find the answer the numbers remaining in the left column are simply added together.

example 2

~~32 × 68~~
~~64 × 34~~
128 × 17
~~256 × 8~~
~~512 × 4~~
~~1024 × 2~~
2048 × 1
―――――――
2176

Activity
Set the children some multiplication sums and suggest they can find the answers by using the ancient Egyptian method.

Discussion
The children could be shown how to do the sum 48 × 27 using the 'long' multiplication method, the method they may well know, and then the Ancient Egyptian method could be demonstrated. Do the children prefer 'long' multiplication or the Ancient Egyptian method. Or do they prefer calculators!

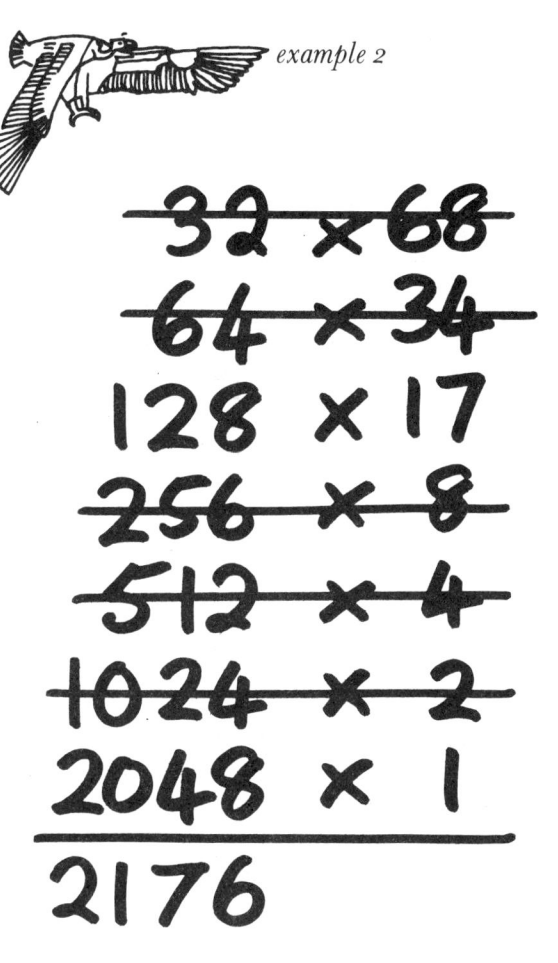

Further activity
Explore the various methods of multiplying from repeated addition to 'long' multiplication. See **Napier's Bones,** *page* **62**.

Additional information
The Binary connection
It will be obvious to children used to binary mathematics that the doubling and halving procedure is based on the binary system.

LATTICE MULTIPLICATION

Time required
30 minutes

Age range
9–13 years

Aim
To investigate an alternative method of multiplication. See also **Napier's Bones**, page **62**.

Organisation
Children can work individually or in pairs.

Equipment
Each child will need
  paper and pencil

Background information
In 15th Century Italy a method of multiplication was resolved on a lattice.

Preparation
Draw a lattice on the blackboard

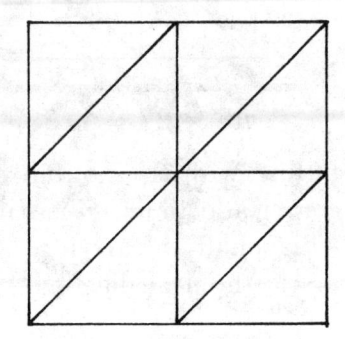

example 1

If you wished to multiply 48 by 27 you would:

a) Draw four squares and then draw in the diagonals from top right to bottom left-hand corner.

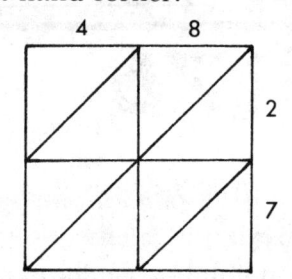

b) Put 48 over the top two squares and 27 to the right of the lattice as shown.

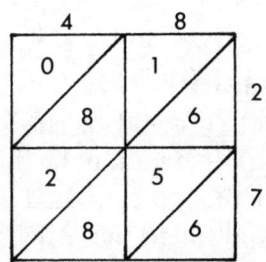

c) Multiply 4 by 2 which equals 8 (written 0/8) and fill in the lattice as shown.

58

48 × 27 = 1296

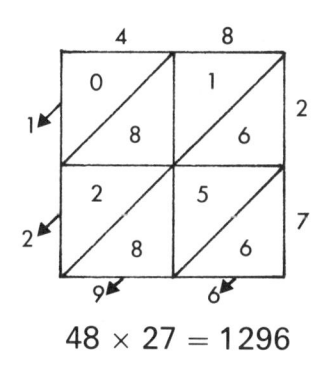

d) Starting with the bottom right-hand corner add the numbers in the lattice diagonally, 'carrying' when necessary to the next diagonal to the left.

example 2

32 × 68 = 2176

Activity

Demonstrate the example and let the children try some multiplication sums using the lattice method. Three or even four digit numbers can be used.

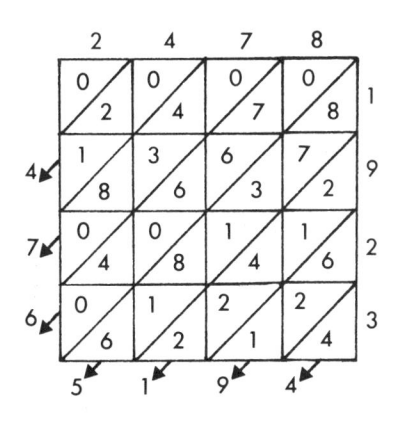

2478 × 1923 = 4,765,194

Further activities

1 Number work on the traditional European method of multiplying and the lesson on **Napier's Bones**.

2 Run a competition to see who can solve 269 × 364 in the shortest time. Half the class should use the lattice method and the other half should use long multiplication.

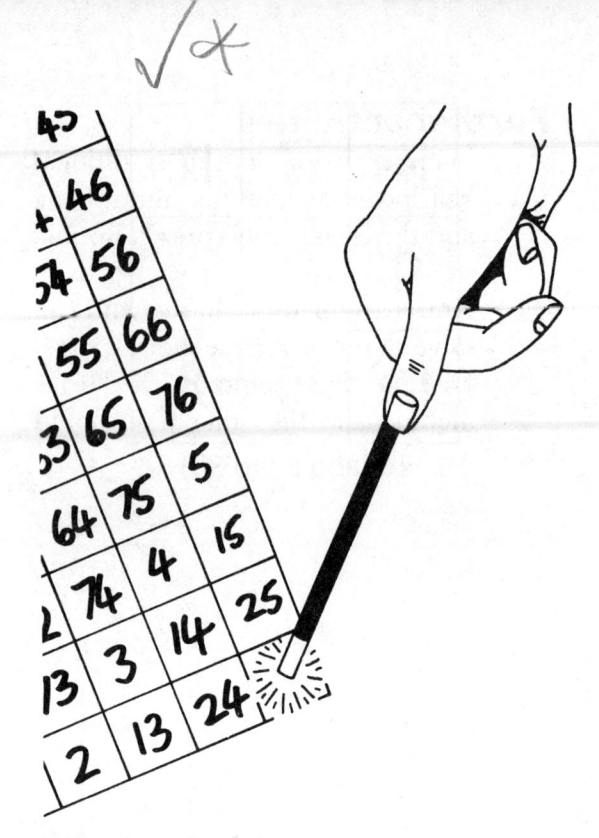

MAGIC SQUARES

Background information

A magic square is a set of numbers arranged in the form of a square, so that the numbers in each row, each column and each diagonal add up to the same total.

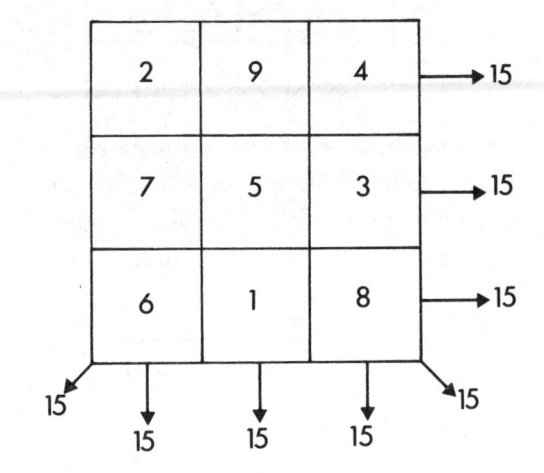

2	9	4
7	5	3
6	1	8

Each row, column and diagonal adds up to 15.

In ancient times such squares were thought to have magical qualities.

The *examples a, b* and *c* used in this lesson all have an odd number of small squares in each side and use consecutive natural numbers beginning with number 1 which is in the middle position on the top line. The formula for filling such a square is given on *page* **118**.

17	24	1	8	15
23	5	7	14	16
4	6	13	20	22
10	12	19	21	3
11	18	25	2	9

each row adds up to 65

example a

Time required
30 minutes

Age range
9–12 years

Aim
To gain experience in addition of numbers and number combinations.

Organisation
Children should work individually or in pairs.

Equipment
Each child will need paper and pencil

30	39	48	1	10	19	28
38	47	7	9	18	27	29
46	6	8	17	26	35	37
5	14	16	25	34	36	45
13	15	24	33	42	44	4
21	23	32	41	43	3	12
22	31	40	49	2	11	20

each row adds up to 175

example b

14	7	12
9	11	13
10	15	8

(to add up to 33)

47	58	69	80	1	12	23	34	45
57	68	79	9	11	22	33	44	46
67	78	8	10	21	32	43	54	56
77	7	18	20	31	42	53	55	66
6	17	19	30	41	52	63	65	76
16	27	29	40	51	62	64	75	5
26	28	39	50	61	72	74	4	15
36	38	49	60	71	73	3	14	25
37	48	59	70	81	2	13	24	35

each row adds up to 369

example c

1	12	8	13
14	7	11	2
15	6	10	3
4	9	5	16

(to add up to 34)

Discussion
Draw the 3 × 3 square on the blackboard and discuss its magical qualities.

Activity
Draw the following, partly-filled, squares on the board and ask the children to complete them.

Further activities
Each child could make up a square with 'magical' properties, using the formula or not, as the teacher wishes. If successful he can then leave out carefully selected numbers and give the square to a neighbour to solve.

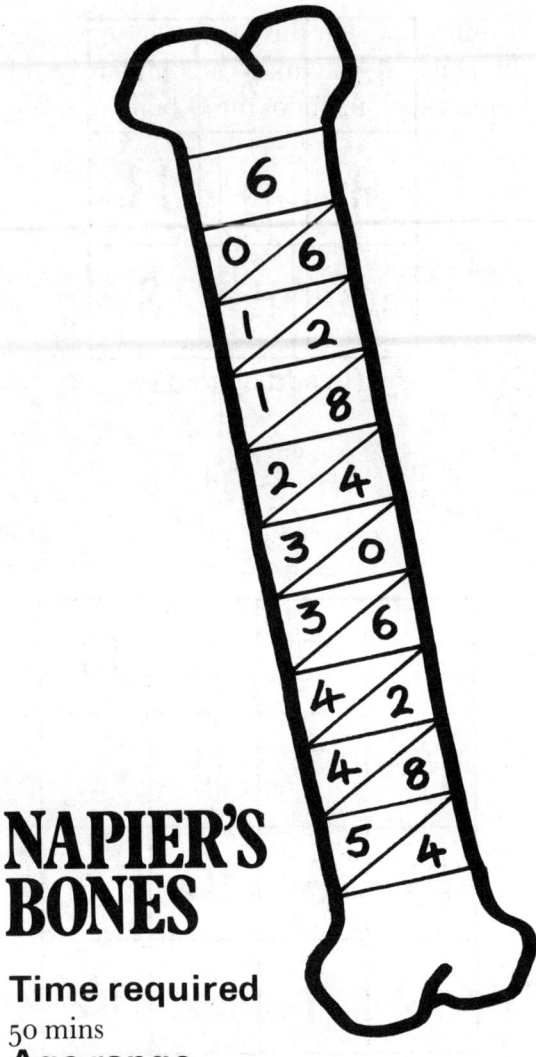

NAPIER'S BONES

Time required
50 mins

Age range
9–12 years

Aim
To investigate simplified methods of multiplication.

(See also **Lattice Multiplication**, page **58**).

Organisation
Children to work individually.

Equipment
Each child will need squared paper, preferably cm² and ideally mounted on light card ruler, pencil and scissors

Background information
Napier's Bones were invented in the 17th century by John Napier, the man responsible for logarithms and the decimal point. The original number columns were in fact cut on bone – hence their name.

Preparation
Draw two bones on the blackboard, the × (times) bone and the **6** bone (or any other bone).

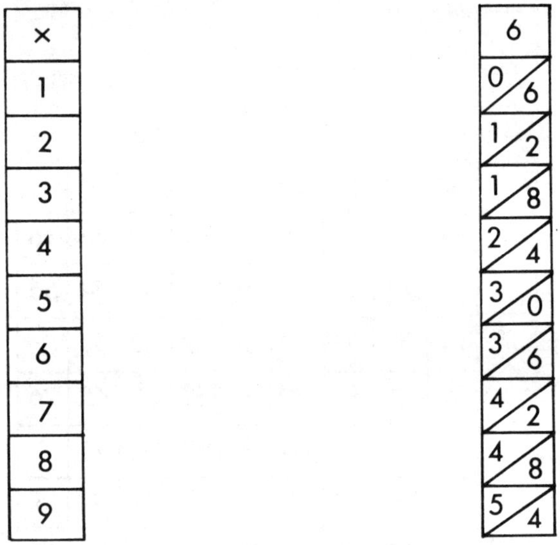

Activity 1
The children should make the two bones from squared paper, using their knowledge of tables to fill in the numbers.

Discussion
The children will soon see that if the two bones are put side by side, the following information can be read off.

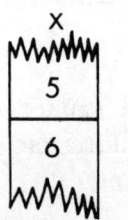

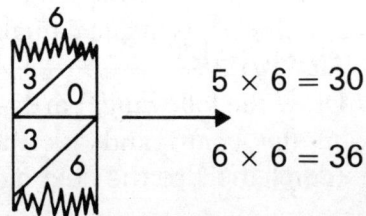

$5 \times 6 = 30$

$6 \times 6 = 36$

Activity 2
Ask the children to make another bone, say the **4**.

Further discussion
Show the children how to read the following

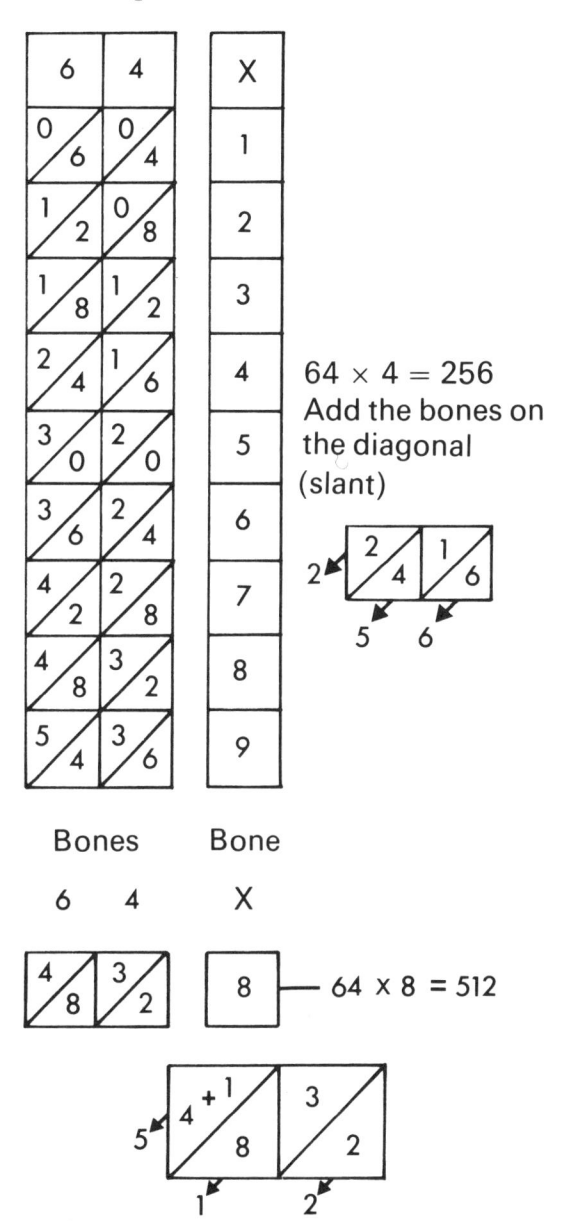

6	4	X
0/6	0/4	1
1/2	0/8	2
1/8	1/2	3
2/4	1/6	4
3/0	2/0	5
3/6	2/4	6
4/2	2/8	7
4/8	3/2	8
5/4	3/6	9

Bones   Bone
6   4   X

64 × 4 = 256
Add the bones on the diagonal (slant)

2 ← 2/4 1/6
    ↓ ↓
    5 6

4/8 3/2   8 — 64 × 8 = 512

5 ← 4+1/8 3/2
    ↓ ↓
    1 2

(carry the 1 to the next diagonal)

If time allows on this or another occasion the children may make a complete set of bones which includes the **O** bone.

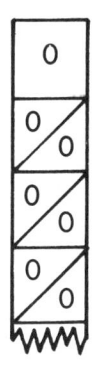

If the children wish to find the solution to 6 × 99, or a similar problem, by this method, then two sets of bones will be required, *ie* they will have to make two **9** bones.

See lesson on **Lattice Multiplication,** *page* **58**.

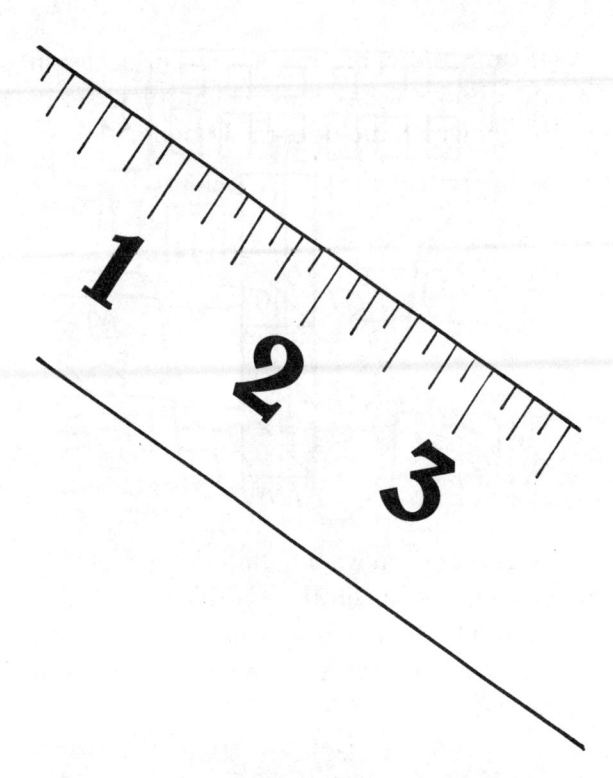

NOMOGRAMS

Time required
30 minutes
Age range
8–11 years
Aim
To show the associative properties of addition and subtraction.
Organisation
Children should work individually.
Equipment
    blackboard
    board ruler
    chalk

Each child will need
    a piece of paper or card
    a pencil
    a ruler

Background information
If a ruler or a strip of paper is passed accurately between any number on line A and any number on line C on the following diagram the total of the two numbers will appear on the middle line.

The ruler can be used to subtract two numbers by joining a number on line A to a number on line B. B minus A gives the answer on line C.

Preparation
Draw the diagram or a part of it on the blackboard. AB *must* equal BC.

Activity
Ask the children to draw this diagram making the spaces along the top and bottom at least 1 cm (2 cm is better), and the distances AB and BC at least 2 cm each. The central numbers must be as close to the points on the central line as possible. It is necessary to stress the need for accuracy and the ruler work involved is itself a valuable exercise.

Discussion
Ask the children if they can discover how to use the diagram as a calculator for addition and subtraction.

Further activities
The teacher could ask the children to solve some problems using this 'calculator' and then encourage them to work out their own and use the strip for checking. For bigger calculations longer strips could be made or steps enlarged to go up in 5s or 10s. Let the children experiment to see what happens when the gap between lines B and C is double that from A to B.

65

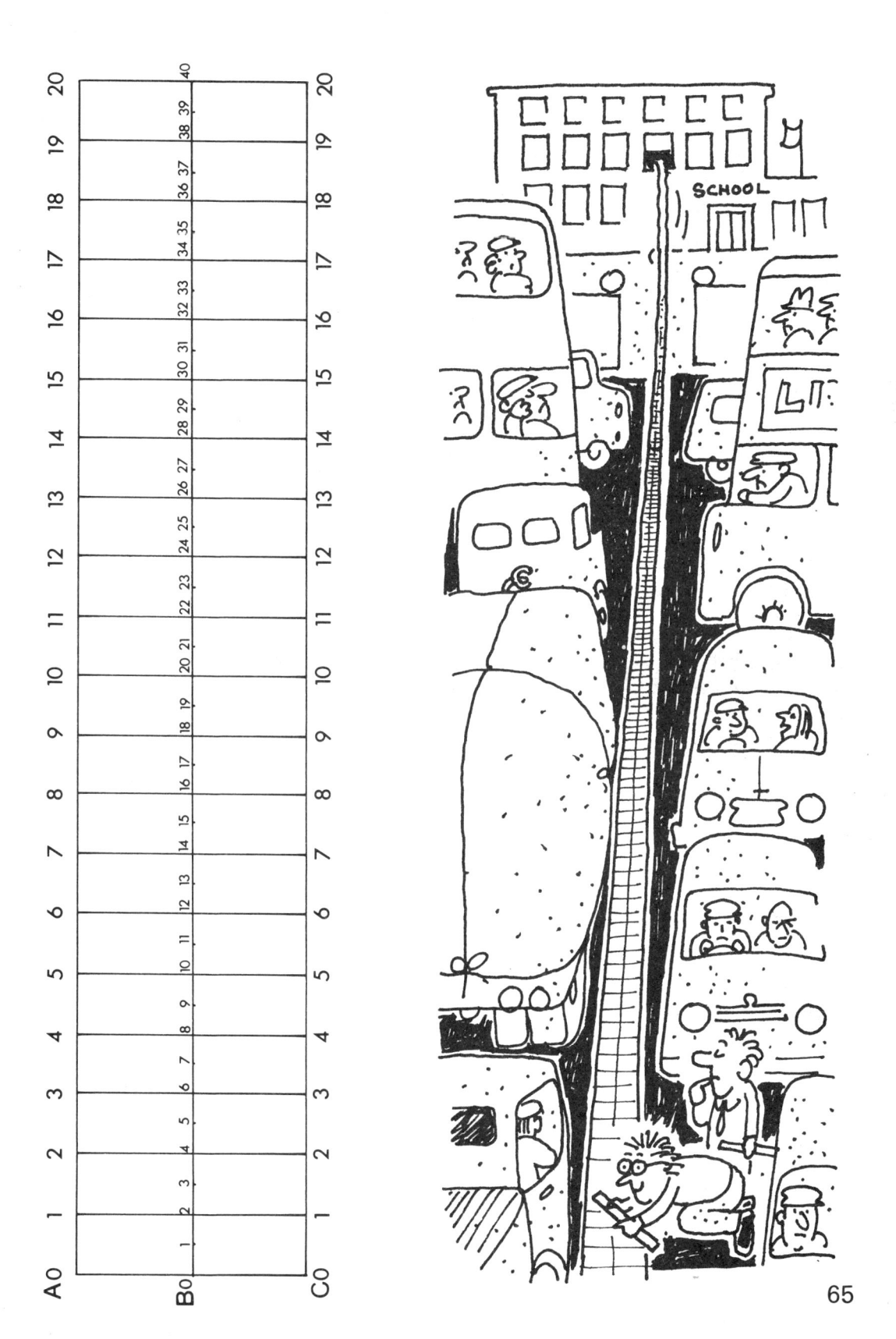

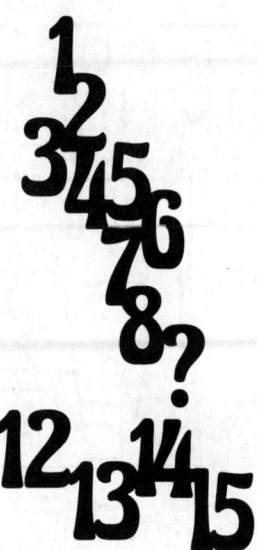

NUMBER COMBINATION SQUARE

Preparation
Draw the following diagram on the blackboard

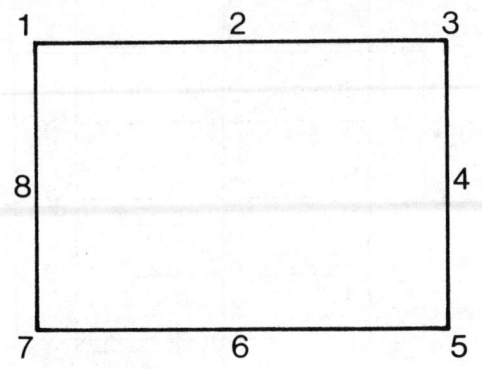

```
1      2      3
┌─────────────┐
│             │
8│             │4
│             │
└─────────────┘
7      6      5
```

Discussion
Explain to the children that by rearranging the numbers it is possible for the numbers to add up to a total of 12 on each side.

Activity
The children should draw the rectangle and rearrange the numbers to add up to 12. This can be repeated with the numbers adding up to 13, 14 and 15. (The children could try 16 but this is impossible.)

Time required
30 minutes

Age range
9–12 years

Aim
To gain experience in addition and number combinations.

Organisation
Children to work individually.

Equipment
Each child will need paper and pencil

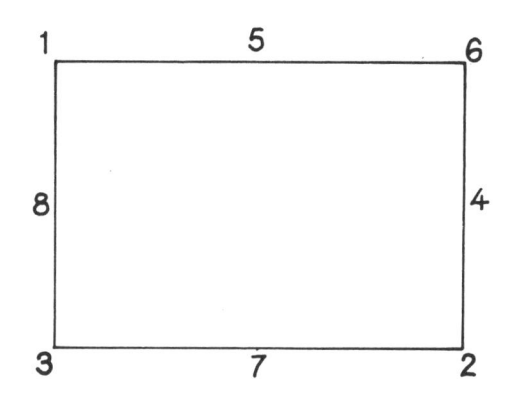

Solutions

```
  1      5      6
   ┌────────────┐
 8 │            │ 4
   │            │
   └────────────┘
  3      7      2
```
total 12

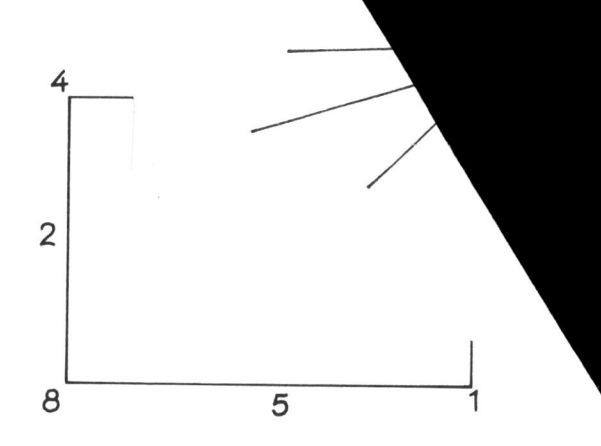

```
  4
  ┌──┐
  │  │
2 │  │
  │  └──────────────┐
  │                 │
  └─────────────────┘ 1
  8        5
```
total 14

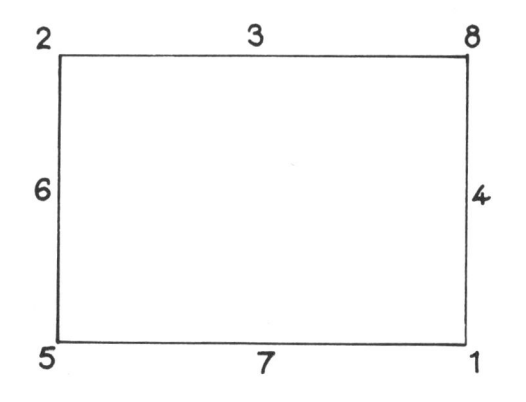

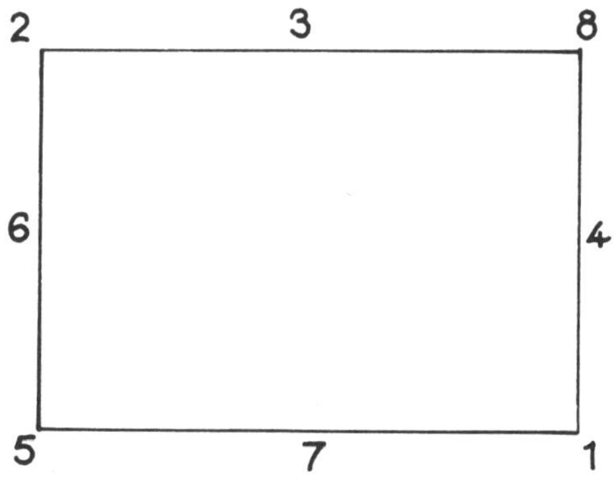

```
  2      3      8
   ┌────────────┐
 6 │            │ 4
   │            │
   └────────────┘
  5      7      1
```
total 13

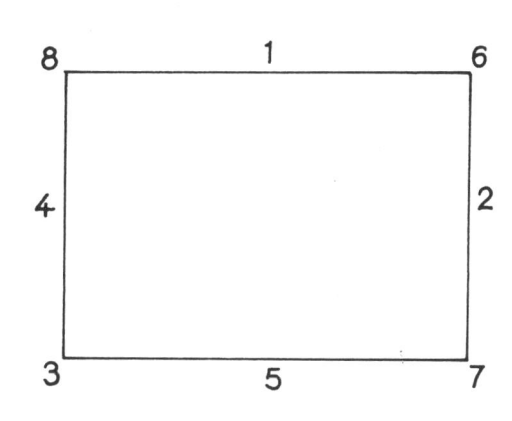

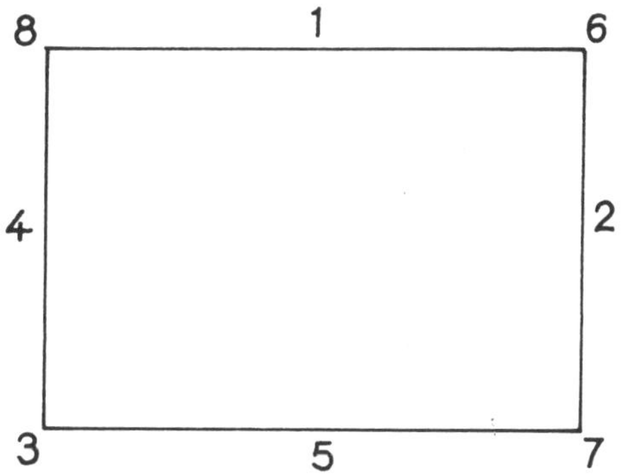

```
  8      1      6
   ┌────────────┐
 4 │            │ 2
   │            │
   └────────────┘
  3      5      7
```
total 15

Intersecting lines

Background information

Triangular numbers are those numbers which can be arranged in the shape of triangles.

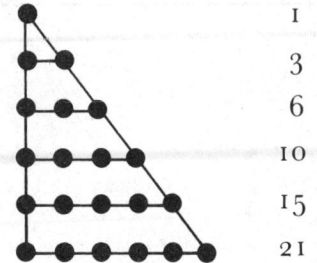

```
•                    1
• •                  3
• • •                6
• • • •             10
• • • • •           15
• • • • • •         21
```

By noting the difference between each consecutive pair of triangular numbers in the sequence it can be shown how the sequence continues.

triangular numbers

$$1 - 3 - 6 - 10 - 15 - 21 - 28 - 36$$
$$\ \ 2\ \ \ 3\ \ \ 4\ \ \ 5\ \ \ \ 6\ \ \ \ 7\ \ \ \ 8\ \ \ \ 9$$

number of intersecting straight lines

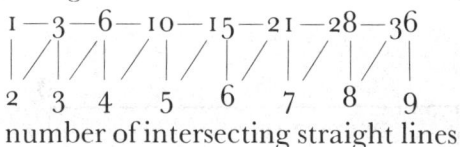

The sequence set out in this form also shows clearly that 2 intersecting straight lines will have 1 point of intersection, 3 intersecting straight lines will have 3 points of intersection, 4 intersecting straight lines will have 6 points of intersection and so on.

Time required
20 minutes

Age range
10–12 years

Aim
To introduce the triangular number sequence.

Organisation
Children to work individually.

Equipment
Each child will need
    paper and pencil
    a ruler

Preparation
On the blackboard the children can be shown that to cross two straight lines is very simple, as it is to cross 3 or 4 straight lines making sure that every line crosses every other line.

Activity 1
Ask the children to copy the shapes from the board and then try to draw 5 straight lines all crossing each other.

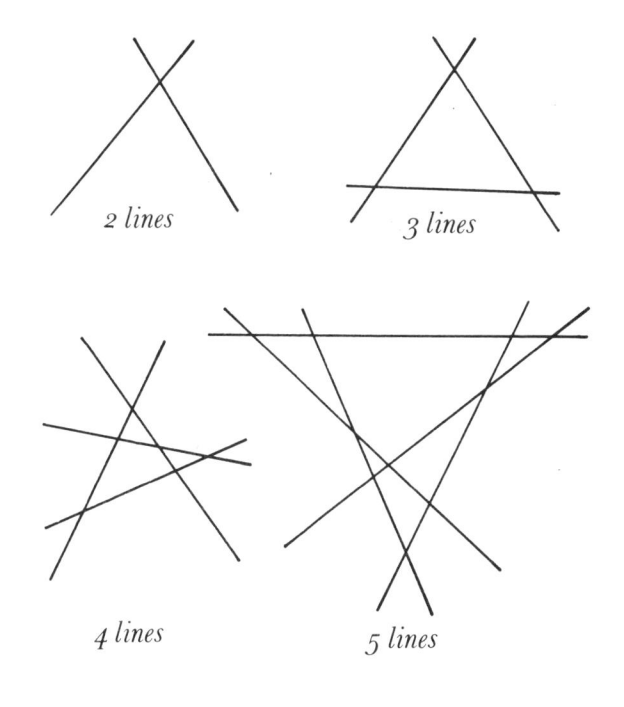

2 lines

3 lines

4 lines

5 lines

It is necessary to ask the children to cross the lines at different points on each line.

example

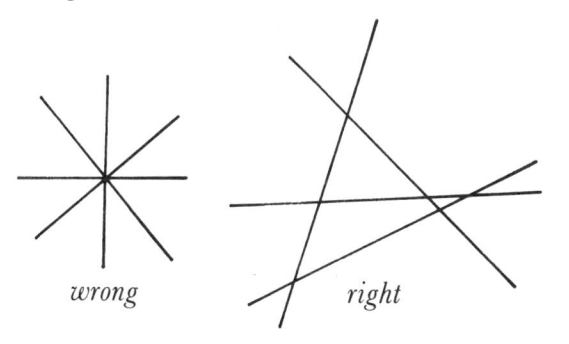

wrong   *right*

Discussion
By looking at the four drawings it can be seen that there are (at the most) the following points of intersection in each of the drawings:

2 lines can have only	1 point of intersection
3 lines can have	3 points of intersection
4 lines can have	6 points of intersection
5 lines can have	10 points of intersection

Activity 2
After counting how many intersections they have on their drawings ask the children to draw 6 straight lines with as many intersections as possible. (There can be as many as 15 points of intersection.)

It can be explained that the number of points of intersection relate to triangular numbers. The children could be asked to guess what would be the most points of intersection in a drawing using seven straight lines (*answer 21*).

The children could then attempt to draw 7 straight lines with 21 intersections. They should be advised to make a large drawing. Perhaps they could number each intersection.

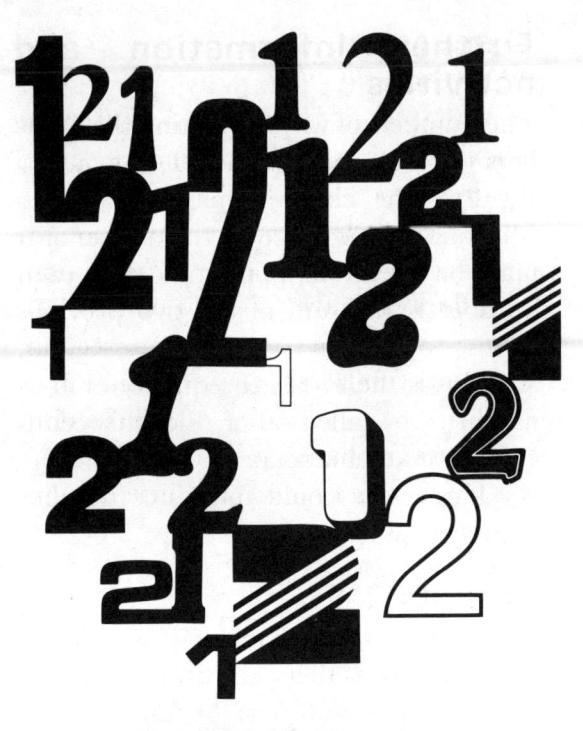

ONES AND TWOS

Time required
20 minutes
Age range
8–11 years
Aim
To extend knowledge of number and number sequences.
Organisation
Work as a class and individually.
Equipment
Each child will need
paper and pencil

Discussion
Show the children on the blackboard that there are two ways of making 2 using only the numbers one and two (obviously $1 = 1$):

$$1 + 1 = 2$$
$$2 = 2$$

Then show the children that there are three ways to make the number 3 using only ones and twos:

$$1 + 1 + 1 = 3$$
$$1 + 2 = 3$$
$$2 + 1 = 3$$

Now ask the children to write the five different ways of writing 4.

Answer

$$1 + 1 + 1 + 1 = 4$$
$$1 + 1 + 2 = 4$$
$$1 + 2 + 1 = 4$$
$$2 + 1 + 1 = 4$$
$$2 + 2 = 4$$

Then ask the children to work out how many different ways there are to make 5 using ones and twos (*answer* 8). This can be repeated for 6 and 7 (*answers* 13, 21).

$$5$$
$$1 + 1 + 1 + 1 + 1$$
$$1 + 1 + 1 + 2$$
$$1 + 1 + 2 + 1$$
$$1 + 2 + 1 + 1$$
$$2 + 1 + 1 + 1$$
$$1 + 2 + 2$$
$$2 + 2 + 1$$
$$2 + 1 + 2$$

6

1 + 1 + 1 + 1 + 1 + 1
1 + 1 + 1 + 1 + 2
1 + 1 + 1 + 2 + 1
1 + 1 + 2 + 1 + 1
1 + 2 + 1 + 1 + 1
2 + 1 + 1 + 1 + 1
1 + 1 + 2 + 2
2 + 2 + 1 + 1
2 + 1 + 2 + 1
1 + 2 + 1 + 2
1 + 2 + 2 + 1
2 + 1 + 1 + 2
2 + 2 + 2

7

1 + 1 + 1 + 1 + 1 + 1 + 1
1 + 1 + 1 + 1 + 1 + 2
1 + 1 + 1 + 1 + 2 + 1
1 + 1 + 2 + 1 + 1 + 1
1 + 1 + 1 + 2 + 1 + 1
1 + 2 + 1 + 1 + 1 + 1
2 + 1 + 1 + 1 + 1 + 1
2 + 2 + 1 + 1 + 1
2 + 1 + 2 + 1 + 1
2 + 1 + 1 + 2 + 1
2 + 1 + 1 + 1 + 2
1 + 2 + 1 + 1 + 2
1 + 1 + 2 + 1 + 2
1 + 1 + 1 + 2 + 2
1 + 1 + 2 + 2 + 1
1 + 2 + 2 + 1 + 1
1 + 2 + 1 + 2 + 1
2 + 2 + 2 + 1
2 + 2 + 1 + 2
2 + 1 + 2 + 2
1 + 2 + 2 + 2

Further information and activities

The numbers of ways of writing the numbers 1–7 form the sequence 1, 2, 3, 5, 8, 13, 21. The children may be able to continue the sequence for themselves or it may be useful to point out that each number is the sum of the two previous terms: $0+1=1$, $1+2=3$, $2+3=5$ ... This is the *Fibonacci* sequence (Fib-o-na-chi), so called after the thirteenth century mathematician.

This lesson could introduce number sequences as a topic.

Background information

The odds against any two people placing eight letters in the same order are 40,320 to 1. In other words there are 40,320 ways of ordering the letters.

The possible number of permutations can be found as follows:

If there are two items, A and B, they can be placed either AB or BA or $1 \times 2 = 2$ permutations.

Three items, A, B, C, can be placed in the following six ways A B C, A C B, B A C, B C A, C B A, C A B or $1 \times 2 \times 3 = 6$ permutations.

Four items, A B C D can be placed thus

ABCD	ABDC	ACBD
ACDB	ADBC	ADCB
BACD	BADC	BCAD
BCDA	BDAC	BDCA
CABD	CADB	CBAD
CBDA	CDAB	CDBA
DABC	DACB	DBAC
DBCA	DCAB	DCBA

or $1 \times 2 \times 3 \times 4 = 24$ permutations.

Five items give $1 \times 2 \times 3 \times 4 \times 5 = 120$ permutations and so on.

WHAT MAKES A GOOD PUPIL?

Time required
30 minutes

Age range
10–13 years

Aim
To explore the realities of permutation.

Organisation
The children can work individually.

Equipment
Each child will need paper and pencil

Preparation
Write on the blackboard or on a large sheet of paper the following list of qualities which could be considered to make a good pupil:

A   Intelligence
B   Hard working
C   Brings teacher presents
D   Quietness
E   Shows responsibility
F   Politeness
G   Neat worker
H   Well dressed

Have your own choice of order written on a piece of paper but kept out of sight.

Discussion
Ask the children if they have seen competitions on cereal packets and in newspapers and magazines where a number of items must be placed in the correct order. Tell the children that you are having a competition to decide what makes a good pupil. Tell them that your list in the correct order is going to be kept secret until they have finished.

Activity
Ask the children to write the numbers 1–8 down on their piece of paper and then to place the letters from the list in the correct order. If they consider that bringing the teacher presents is the most important thing that makes a good pupil then they are to write the letter C by number 1, and so on. It may be a good idea to progress towards dealing with all eight letters by starting first with three, then four or five. This demonstrates well the increasing number of possible permutations.

Discussion
Check to see if any children have the same order as yourself. This is unlikely, but if they have tell them what the chance is of this happening. Show them the possible combinations using A B and A B C and ask them to work out the odds using A B C D. You can finish by showing them the easy formula shown above.

Further information and activities
Children could make a graph to show the class choices of first position. Further work could be done by children working out the odds of throwing the same number on a die twice running, three times running, and so on.

THE DERBY

Background information
When a die is thrown to see which number is the first to be turned up six times, any one of the six numbers can win as they all have the same chance with the odds of 1 to 5.

Preparation
Write across the bottom of the blackboard the numbers 1–6.

Discussion
Tell the children there is going to be a race. Choose six children for the six numbers. They will take it in turns to throw the die.

Activity 1
Mark an X above the number turned up each time the die is thrown and see which number is the first to get six crosses above it. A race can be made out of the situation.

Activity 2
Now write the numbers 1–12 on the board and choose twelve children to represent the numbers. Tell the children that two dice are to be used. By throwing the two dice, and adding their totals, score as in the first race.

Discussion
It will soon be obvious that 1 will be a non-starter. It is most likely that 7 will win, with 6 or 8 having the second best chance. A second 12 runner race can be held if required, but by now some children may be beginning to suspect the 'unfair' advantage. After the races the children can be shown why 7 has the best chance by drawing the following matrix on the board.

Time required
30 minutes

Age range
8–11 years

Aim
To demonstrate probability.

Organisation
Children to work as a class and individually.

Equipment
two dice

+	1	2	3	4	5	6
1	2	3	4	5	6	7
2	3	4	5	6	7	8
3	4	5	6	7	8	9
4	5	6	7	8	9	10
5	6	7	8	9	10	11
6	7	8	9	10	11	12

From this matrix it can be seen that 7 can be obtained by 6 different combinations, whereas 2 can only be made if the two 1's are thrown.

    Odds for 7 are 6 to 30 or 1 to 5.
    Odds for 2 are 1 to 35.

Further activities

Discuss the chances of various games from tossing a coin or cutting a pack of cards, to a study of fruit machines.

Curves of pursuit

Time required
30 minutes

Age range
9–13 years

Aim
To show children that some processes are indeterminate.

Organisation
Children can work individually or in pairs but should be in a position to see the blackboard or a large sheet of paper.

Equipment
    a metric rule and chalk for the teacher

Each child needs
    a ruler marked in centimetres
    paper and pencil

Background information
A vertical line marked R at the top and B at the base represents the route run by a rabbit to its burrow. A point D to one side of the line represents a dog wishing to catch the rabbit. Assuming that the dog and the rabbit run at exactly the same speed and that they start running at the same moment, the dog will never catch the rabbit as long as the rabbit is moved each time the dog is moved. The dog at some point may arrive where the rabbit <u>was</u> standing, but the rabbit will meanwhile have moved.

Discussion
Discuss with the children the difference between men and animals; they will mention the obvious ones such as feeding habits, fur, paws, hands. Guide them towards discussing the differences in intelligence. Take dogs as an example. A man's thinking will always go a stage further than that of a dog for a man can always work out in advance, things which will happen in a new situation, but a dog is not capable of doing this.

Preparation
Draw a line, marked at 10 cm intervals, down one side of a blackboard or large sheet of paper, making one end R (rabbit) and the other end B (burrow). These points should be some 60–80 cm apart. Mark a point to one side, D (dog), as in the diagram:

The dog should be nearer to the rabbit and to the burrow than the rabbit is to the burrow to make the demonstration effective.

Ask the children if the dog will catch the rabbit before the rabbit reaches his burrow, assuming that the dog and the rabbit run at exactly the same speed and that the dog and the rabbit start running at the same moment. Lay the metre rule along the board between points D and R and draw a line 10 cm long from D towards R. During this time the rabbit will have run 10 cm from R towards B.

The dog now looks up and sees that the rabbit has run from his original position to position R2, so he changes direction and runs 10 cm towards R2. Meanwhile the rabbit runs another 10 cm to point R3. The dog looks up and changes his course towards R3 – and so on. (In actual fact the dog would probably keep his eye on the rabbit but would always run <u>at</u> the rabbit.)

Activity

Let the children try this on their paper using moves of 1 cm to see if the dog can catch the rabbit and placing the dog anywhere they like to the side of the straight line.

For a second attempt let the children increase the speed of the dog, so that the dog runs 1½ cm compared to 1 cm for the rabbit.

Further activities

1 Try the same exercise but with the rabbit running around the outside of a circle and the dog starting in the centre.
2 Further work on making curves by using straight lines and going on to curve stitching patterns.
3 Discussion of other comparisons between man and beast such as running speeds.

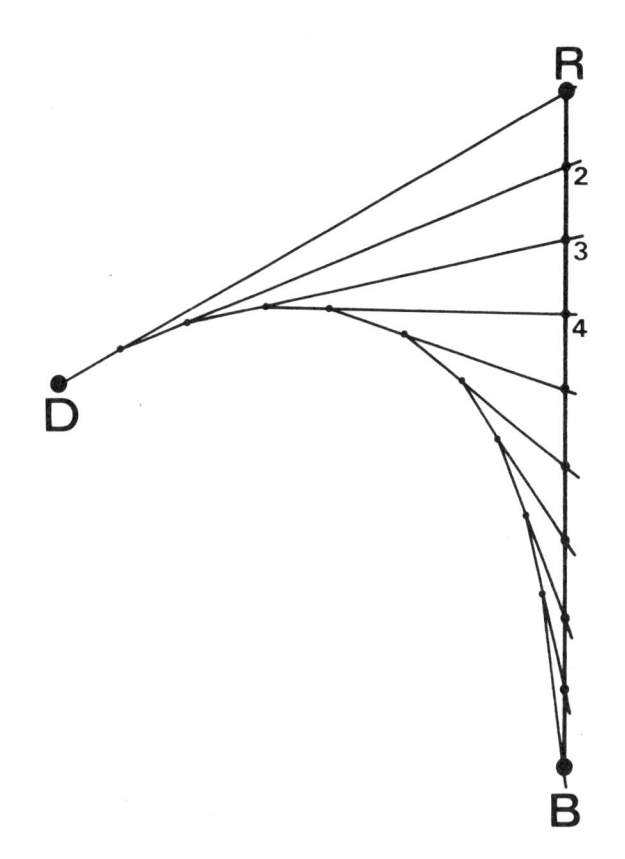

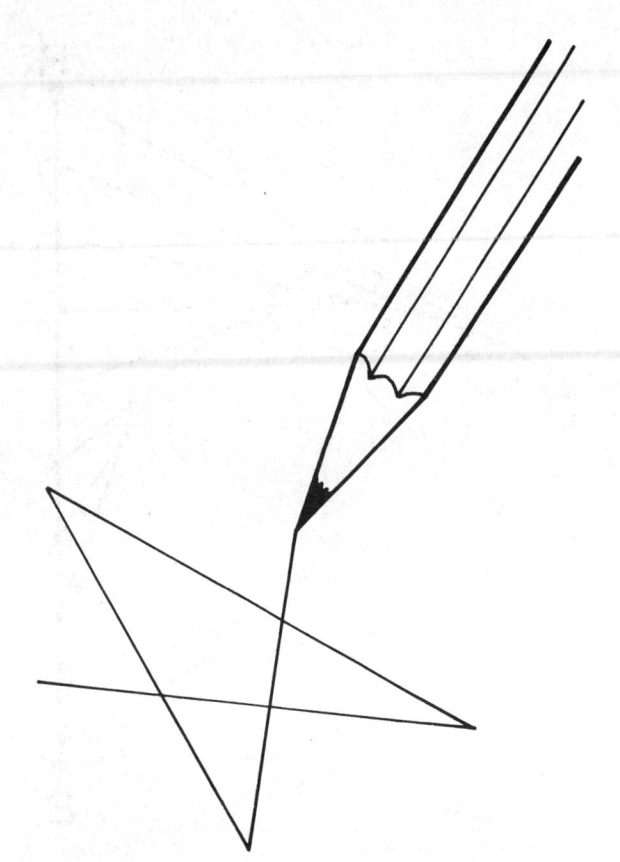

NETWORKS

Background information
In determining whether or not a network can be drawn without taking the pencil off the paper and without going over any line twice, the crucial factor is the number of 3 joints in the network. If there are more than two 3 joints the network cannot be completed without taking the pencil off the paper or going over one line twice. If there are even-numbered joints the lines can be paired off so there can be 'entry and exit'. At odd joints, there will also be a beginning or an end.

Preparation
Draw the following networks on the blackboard.

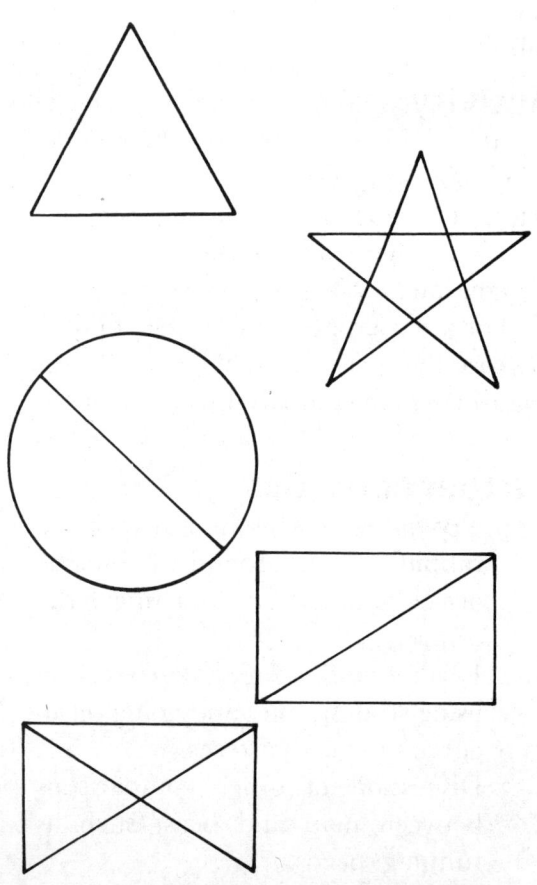

Time required
40 minutes

Age range
9–12 years

Aim
To investigate the properties of certain shapes.

Organisation
Children to work as a class and individually.

Equipment
Each child will need
 paper and pencil
 a coloured pencil or felt pen

Activity

Ask the children to copy these networks from the board and then draw over them with a coloured pencil without taking the pencil off the paper and without going over any line twice. They may need more than one attempt before they are successful.

Now draw the two following networks on the board and ask them to do the same.

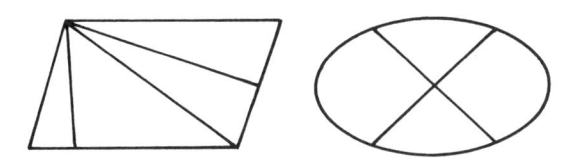

The last two shapes are impossible to do as the children will soon discover.

Discussion

Show the children that there are different types of joints in the drawings:

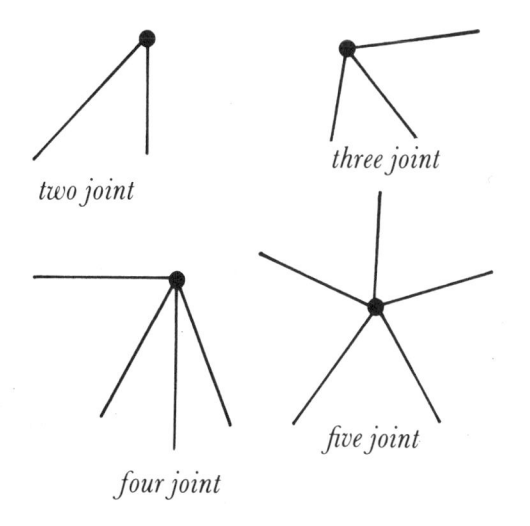

two joint

three joint

four joint

five joint

Look at the networks that can be drawn and count the different types of joints in each. Do this with the two 'impossible' networks as well. Ask the children if they can spot any difference between the types of joint, and number of joints, of those that can be drawn and those that cannot.

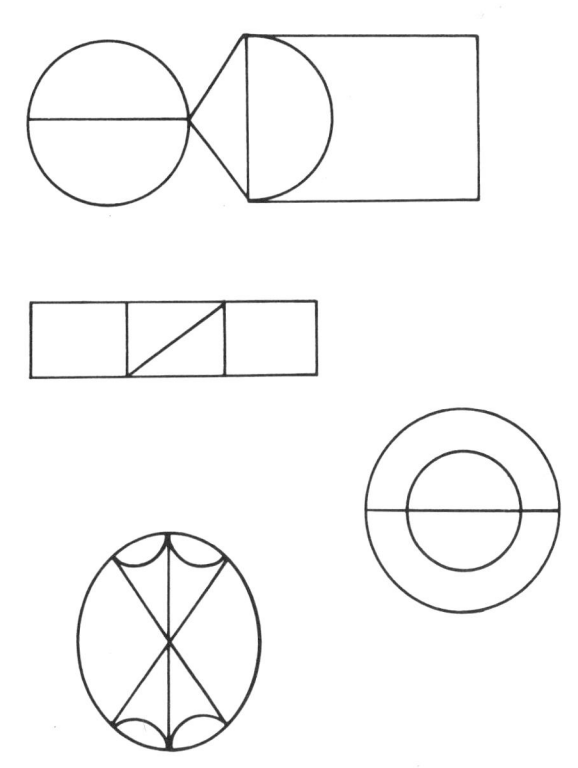

The children can look at these shapes on the board and decide from the joints which can be done and which cannot. They can test their decisions.

Further activities

The practical use of networks can be seen when planning delivery routes, looking at local maps and devising walks. The children could have great fun planning such a walk and testing the route they devise.

POLYOMINOES

Background information
Polyominoes are shapes made from squares, the domino being the most well-known. Strangely there is no mathematical formula for the number of distinct polyominoes. There are however 35 different types of hexominoes and 108 different heptominoes, although that number includes the debatable

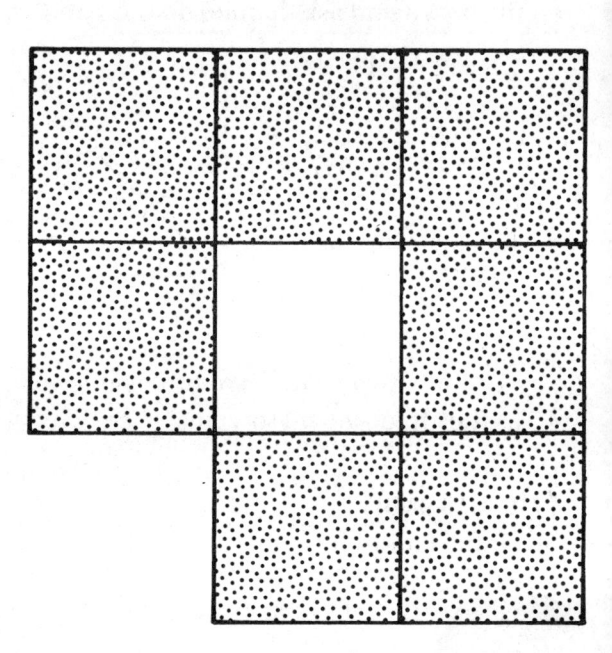

Time required
35 minutes

Age range
9–13 years

Aim
To explore the shapes which can be made out of squares placed in various combinations. *See also* **Pentomino puzzle,** *page* **82.**

Organisation
Children to work individually.

Equipment
Each child will need
- a piece of squared paper (preferably cm²)
- pencils and crayons

Discussion
Ask the children whether they have played dominoes. Discuss the game and the domino shape. What is a monomino? □ a single square What is a tromino? What shapes could they be?

straight tromino   right tromino

Explain that ⌐⌐ is the same as

and they are just in a different position or turned over.

Activity 1

Tell the children that a four square shape is called a tetromino. Ask them to draw the five different tetrominoes on the squared paper. The squares must be joined by the edges. is not acceptable.

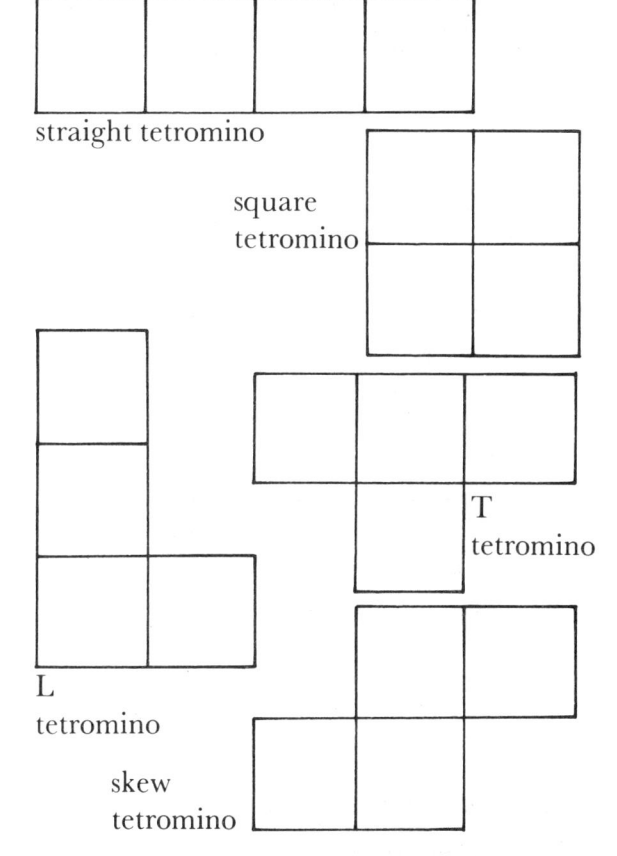

straight tetromino

square tetromino

T tetromino

L tetromino

skew tetromino

Pentominoes

Discussion

Tell the children that the pentomino (5 squares) is a popular polyomino for games, but what are the various shapes and how many are there?

Activity 2

The children should draw the pentominoes on their squared paper. The whole class can later check their results on the blackboard with the teacher.

Further activities

See **Pentomino puzzle**, *page* **82**.

81

Pentomino puzzle

Time required
45 minutes
Age range
9–13 years
Aim
To explore the tessellation of pentominoes. See also **Polyominoes**, *page* 80
Organisation
Children to work individually or in pairs.
Equipment
Each child will need
- a piece of cm squared paper which should ideally be mounted on light card
- paste and a piece of card (optional)
- a pair of scissors
- a pencil

Background information
A tessera was one of the pieces of stone in a Roman mosaic and a small tessera was called a tessella. Tessellation is the fitting together of small flat shapes into 'all over' patterns as on a tiled floor.

Preparation
Draw on the blackboard the only shape that can be made with two squares.

is not acceptable

Draw also the two shapes that can be made using three squares.

this shape is of course only the reverse of

Activity 1
Ask the children to draw on their squared paper, the shapes that can be made using four squares.

These are the five shapes that can be made.

82

Tell the children or, if there is sufficient time, encourage them to discover the fact that twelve different shapes can be made using five squares. Ask them to draw them. These shapes are called pentominoes.

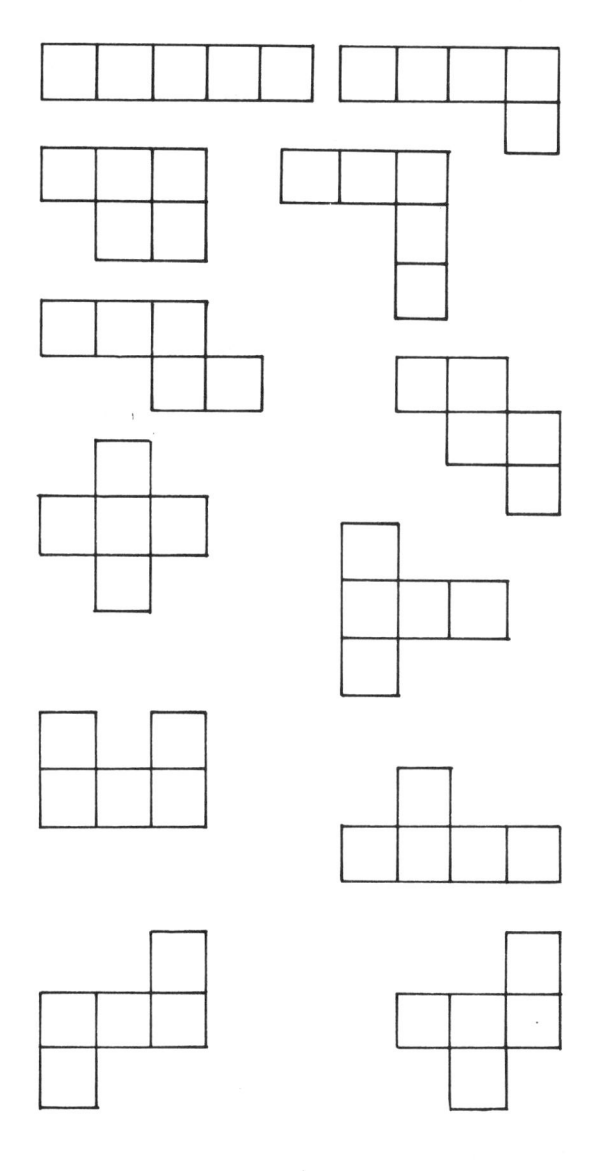

When the children have discovered or have been shown the twelve shapes ask them to cut out the shapes carefully.

Activity 2

Ask the children to construct a 10 cm × 6 cm rectangle using all the shapes. Obviously shapes made of card are easier to handle than paper shapes which tend to blow about and curl. It may sometimes be necessary to start the puzzle for the children to complete. Most children will be interested to learn that there are over 2,000 possible solutions to this puzzle. Here is just one to show it really can be done.

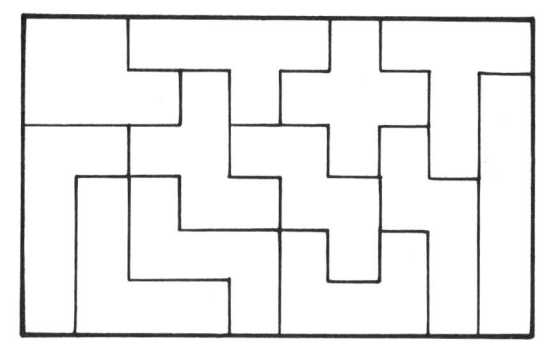

Further activities

If the children have enjoyed solving the 10 cm × 6 cm rectangle they could try rectangles of 3 cm × 20 cm, 4 cm × 15 cm or 5 cm × 12 cm. *See page* **119** for solution. Ask the children to select one of the twelve pentominoes and draw and cut out a dozen or more of the same shape. Use the shape to cover an area, like tiling a floor. The pieces could be coloured with felt pen or crayon and stuck on to large sheets of paper for an attractive wall display.

Ask the children to try using two or even three shapes to cover an area.

This could result in a project which deals with the whole subject of tessellation, from regular and irregular shapes to the tessellation patterns which can be found in nature (pine cones, honeycomb, fish scales etc.).

83

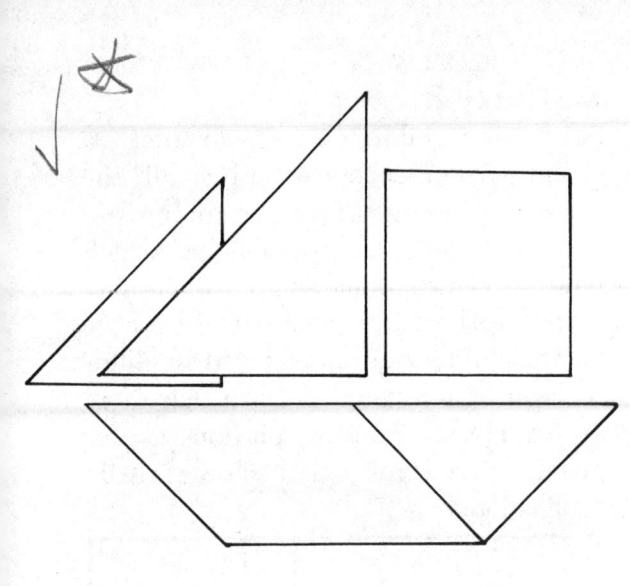

Background information
Tangrams are some of the oldest puzzles in the world. They were popular in China before the birth of Christ.

Preparation
Draw the following diagram on the blackboard.

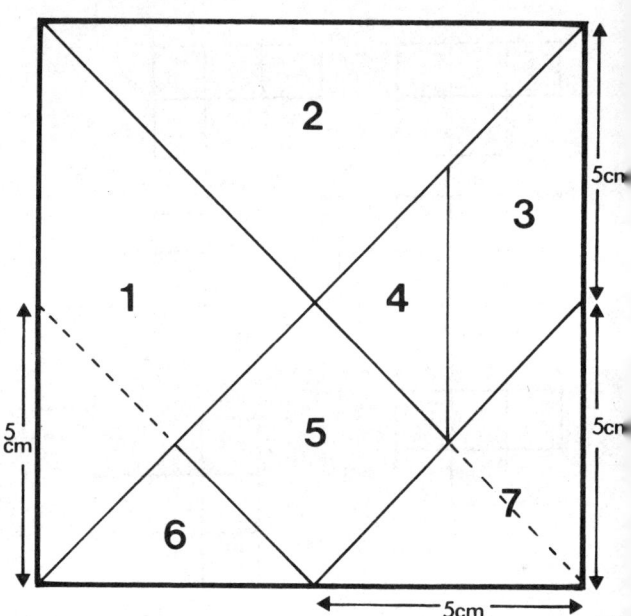

Tangrams

Time required
50 minutes

Age range
9–12 years

Aim
To have fun with mathematical shapes.

Organisation
Children to work individually.

Equipment
Each child will need
- a piece of paper or card
- a pair of scissors
- a pencil
- a ruler

Activity 1
Ask the children to cut their paper or card into a 10 cm × 10 cm square. Then tell them to carefully measure and draw the diagram. Finally, the children are to cut out the seven shapes (do not cut the dotted lines).

Discussion
Talk about the shapes
- 2 large triangles (1 and 2)
- 1 medium-sized triangle (7)
- 2 small triangles (6 and 4)
- 1 parallelogram (3)
- 1 square (5)

Activity 2

Ask the children to use their own pieces to construct the following. This assignment makes a good subject for a class competition.

1. a) a square using two triangles
   b) a parallelogram using the same two triangles
      (both have, of course, the same area).
2. a) a rectangle using any three pieces
   b) a parallelogram using the same three pieces
      (both have the same area: connection between formulae for the two areas should be noted)
3. a parallelogram using any 4 pieces
4. a triangle using any 3 pieces
5. a trapezium using any 3 pieces
6. another trapezium using pieces 3, 4, 5, 6
7. a triangle using pieces 3, 4, 5, 6, 7
8. a large square using all the pieces (the original shape)
9. a large rectangle using all the pieces

See page **120** *for solutions to the constructions.*

Further activities

Make simple pictures using the pieces.

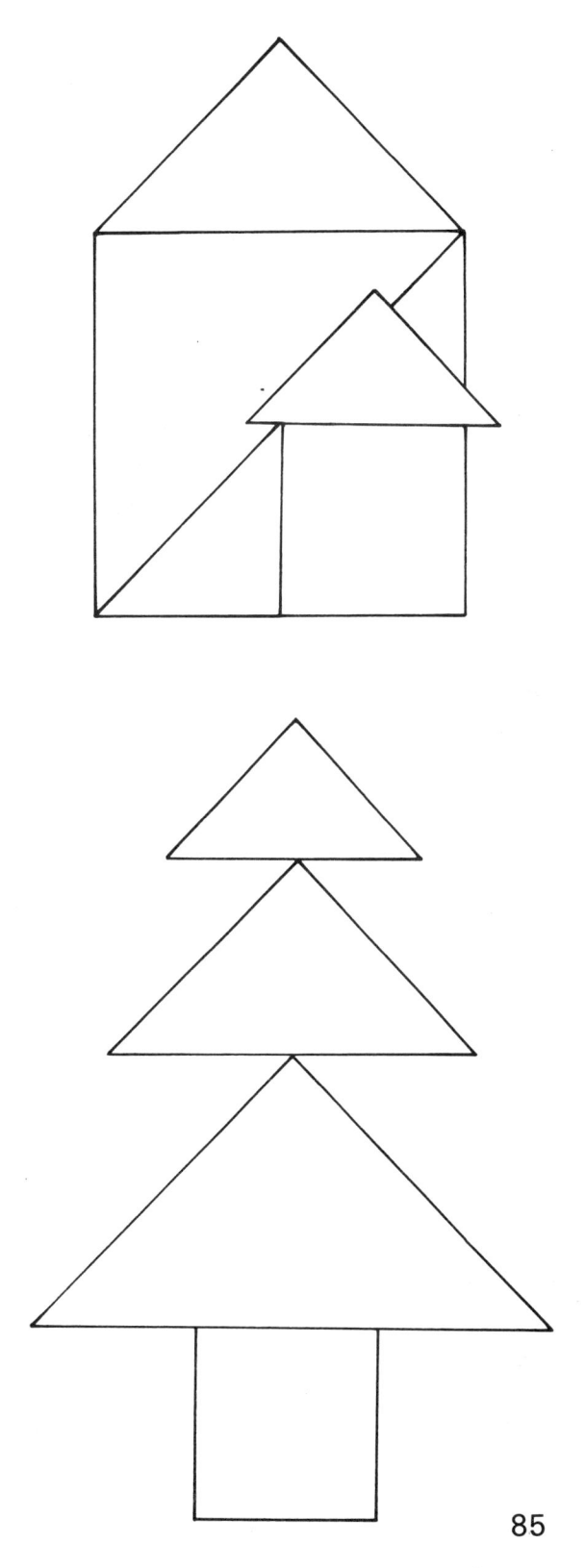

MIRROR REFLECTIONS

Background information
The mirror reflection of ten letters of the alphabet is unchanged. (These letters have a vertical line of symmetry – A, H, I, M, O, T, V, W, X, Y)

With the mirror placed at the base of the letters the mirror reflection of nine letters is unchanged. (These letters have a horizontal line of symmetry – B, C, D, E, H, I, K, O, X)

Preparation
The teacher draws on the blackboard the capital letters A–E.

Discussion
A discussion of the effects of looking into the mirror, reverse images etc. Show the children what the mirror reflection of the capital letters on the board would look like.

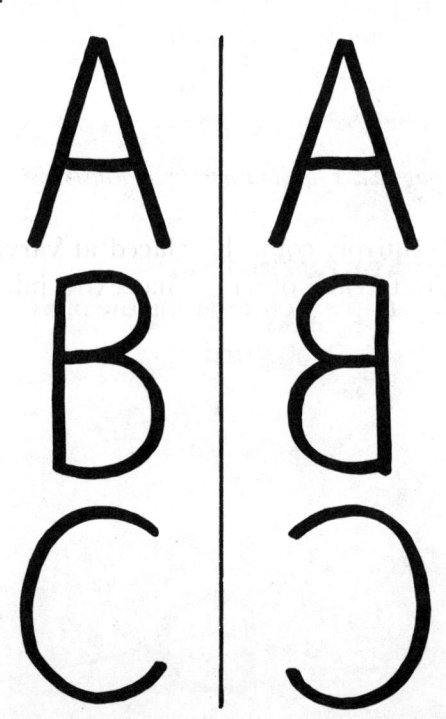

Time required
45 minutes

Age range
8–11 years

Aim
To introduce an aspect of symmetry.

Organisation
Children to work individually.

Equipment
The children will need
- a piece of squared paper
- a pencil
- a mirror (ideally one each if the school has a supply or a larger mirror used by the teacher for demonstration)

Activity 1
The children should draw the capital letters of the alphabet on squared paper and draw their mirror reflections to the side.

Discussion
Ask the children what would be the mirror reflection if the mirror were placed at the base of the letters. Show with examples on the board.

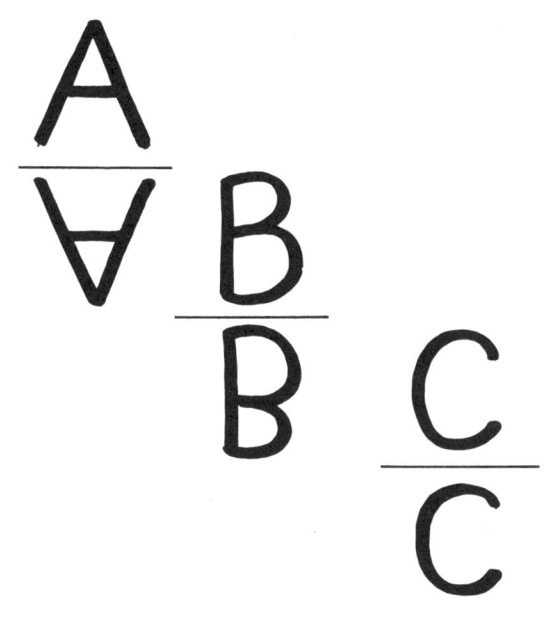

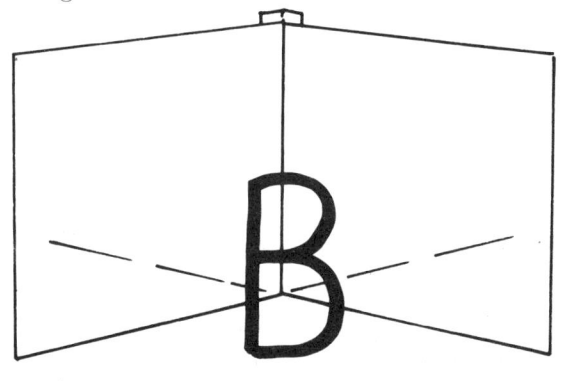

The children could do this with the letters B, H, N and R, to produce different combinations of reflections.

A real test would be to draw a house on the squared paper and reproduce the reflections.

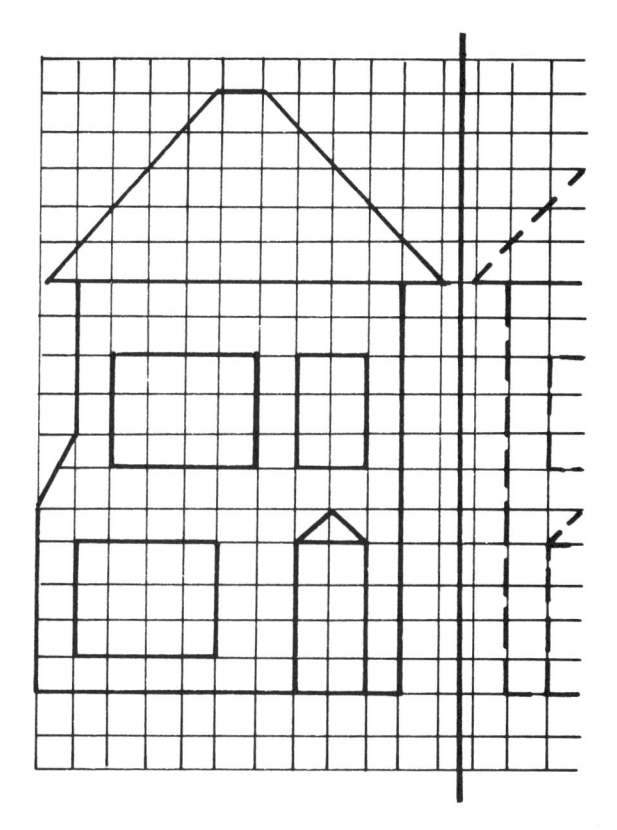

Activity 2
Two mirrors could be placed at varying angles to each other so that extra mirror images are obtained.

Further activities
This lesson may be used to introduce mathematical symmetry or to begin a discussion on symmetry in nature.

87

ANYBALL

Time required
10 minutes

Age range
9–13 years

Aim
To involve children in a physical activity which uses a variety of skills.

Organisation
This is a team game to be played in a hall or gymnasium or out of doors on playground or field. The teams can be of any size from 3 to 20. The game can be organised as a knockout tournament, or as a game which involves the whole class. If the numbers are large (more than 10 a side) and the game has to be played indoors then it may be better to play the substitute type game suggested at the end of this lesson.

Equipment
two goals made up of rostra blocks or tables turned over so that the tops are turned towards the pitch
two medium-sized balls

Rules
1 As the title suggests, once the teacher has thrown the balls into play, they may be kicked, headed, punched, hit with the flat of the hand or thrown.
2 If a player holds the ball in his hands
   a) no other player may touch him
   b) he must not move until he has released the ball
   c) he must release the ball within 3 seconds.
3 A goal is scored when a ball strikes the table top – having been propelled by any of the methods listed.
4 A goal scorer must immediately run and stand behind his own goal.
5 The first team with all players standing behind their own goal is the winner.

Further information and activities
1 The game may, of course, be played with only one ball or, indeed, with as many as 6.
2 For larger numbers in an enclosed space half the team should sit out as 'substitutes'. As soon as a goal is scored, the goal scorer should go and touch one of his team substitutes before going behind his own goal. The substitute then runs on and plays, staying in the game until he too scores.
3 Can be used to develop skills for major ball games.

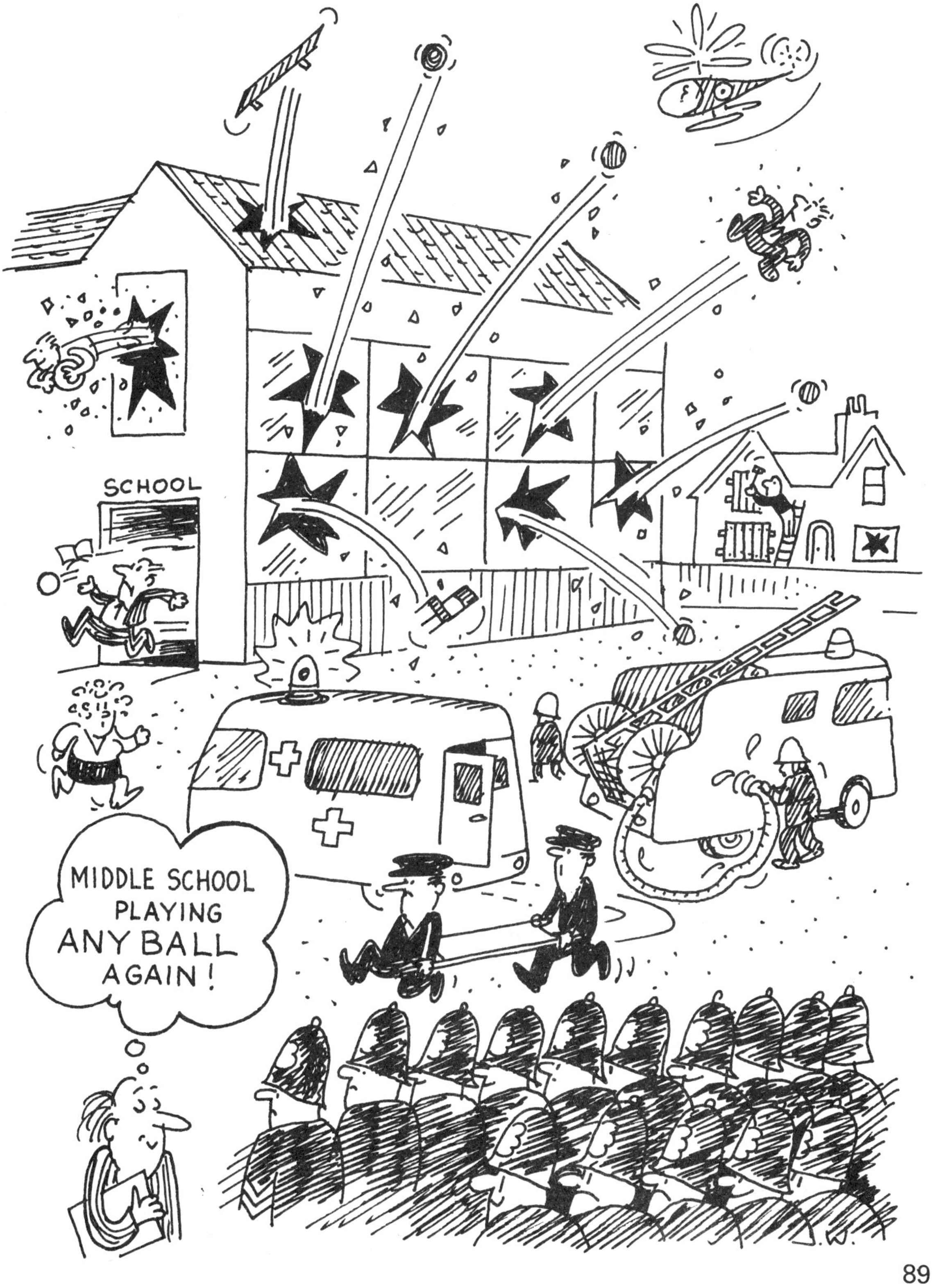
SCHOOL
MIDDLE SCHOOL PLAYING ANY BALL AGAIN!

CHAIRBALL

Preparation
Set the court out as shown.

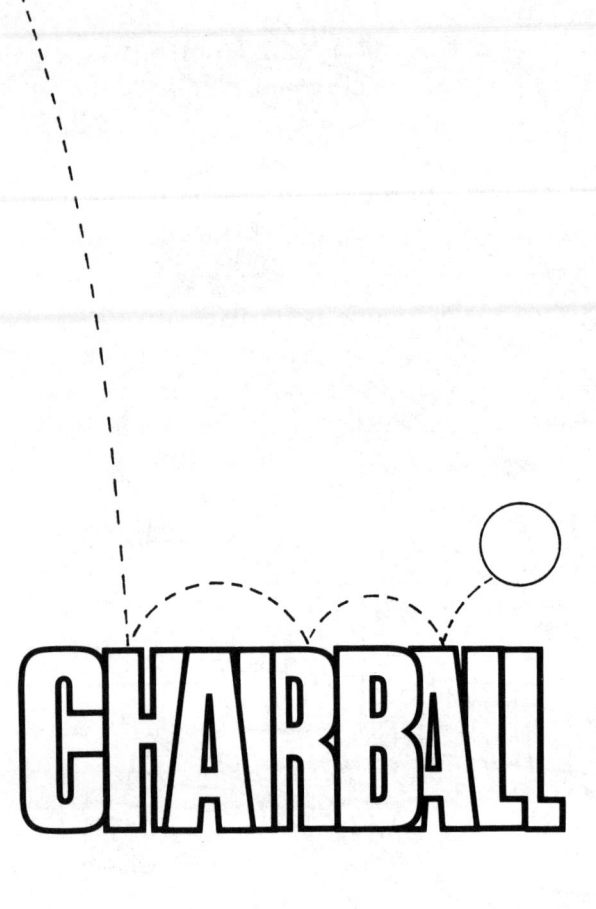

Time required
25 minutes
Age range
7–12 years
Aim
To develop team co-operation and to provide catching practice.
Organisation
The class should be divided into teams of five or six children.
Equipment
    Gymnasium/Hall
    two chairs
    two gymnastic mats
    large ball
    bibs or bands

MAT

CHAIR

Before the game starts the teams should line up as follows:

Rules
1. The object of the game is to get the ball to your team member sitting on the chair.
2. The first team to get 3 or 5 (depending on the time) passes to the team member sitting on the chair are the winners.
3. The game is started with the ball being thrown high into the air in the centre of the pitch by the teacher. After every score the game is restarted with a 'throw up'.
4. Running with the ball is not allowed; no kicking or punching of the ball allowed; no player to step on either mat; blocking and intercepting of the ball is allowed but not knocking the ball out of an opponent's hand; the final pass must be directly into the hands of the player on the chair (no bouncing or rebounding off a wall); the player sitting on the chair must remain seated at all times.
5. Following a foul, possession of the ball passes to the other team.

Activity
Play the game in heats with a loser's final and a winner's final.

Hand Hockey

Time required
20 minutes – (each game may only last 5 or 6 minutes, with a 'change ends' at half-time).

Age range
7–13 years

Aim
To co-ordinate passing skills.

Organisation
This is a team game for school hall or gymnasium. The size of the teams will vary with the amount of space available and the number of children in the class. The ideal size of a team is about 5 children, but it can be played by 2 against 2, up to about 10 against 10. A class of 30 to 40 children should be split into 4, 5, 6, 7 or 8 teams and then played off against each other in a knockout competition (always making sure that the early losers get the chance of another game later) or a league competition, where each team plays against each of the others.

Equipment
two benches (or something similar) for use as goals, laid on their sides at each end of the hall
coloured bands if possible
a medium-sized plastic ball

Activity
The game is played with the following rules:
1. The game is started with a ball being rolled into play by the teacher.
2. The ball must only be played with a flat hand (not punched, and only with one hand).
3. The ball must not be picked up or kicked.
4. If the ball is intentionally picked up, kicked, punched, played with two hands or blocked with the body a free hit is awarded to the opposing side.
5. A goal is scored when the ball strikes the front face of the bench. Any member of the team may score but the children will soon realise that they must be as ready to defend as to attack.

Other information and activities
This is a useful game for teaching passing, moving into spaces and basic teamwork. It can also be useful when games have to be played in the hall or gym because of bad weather.

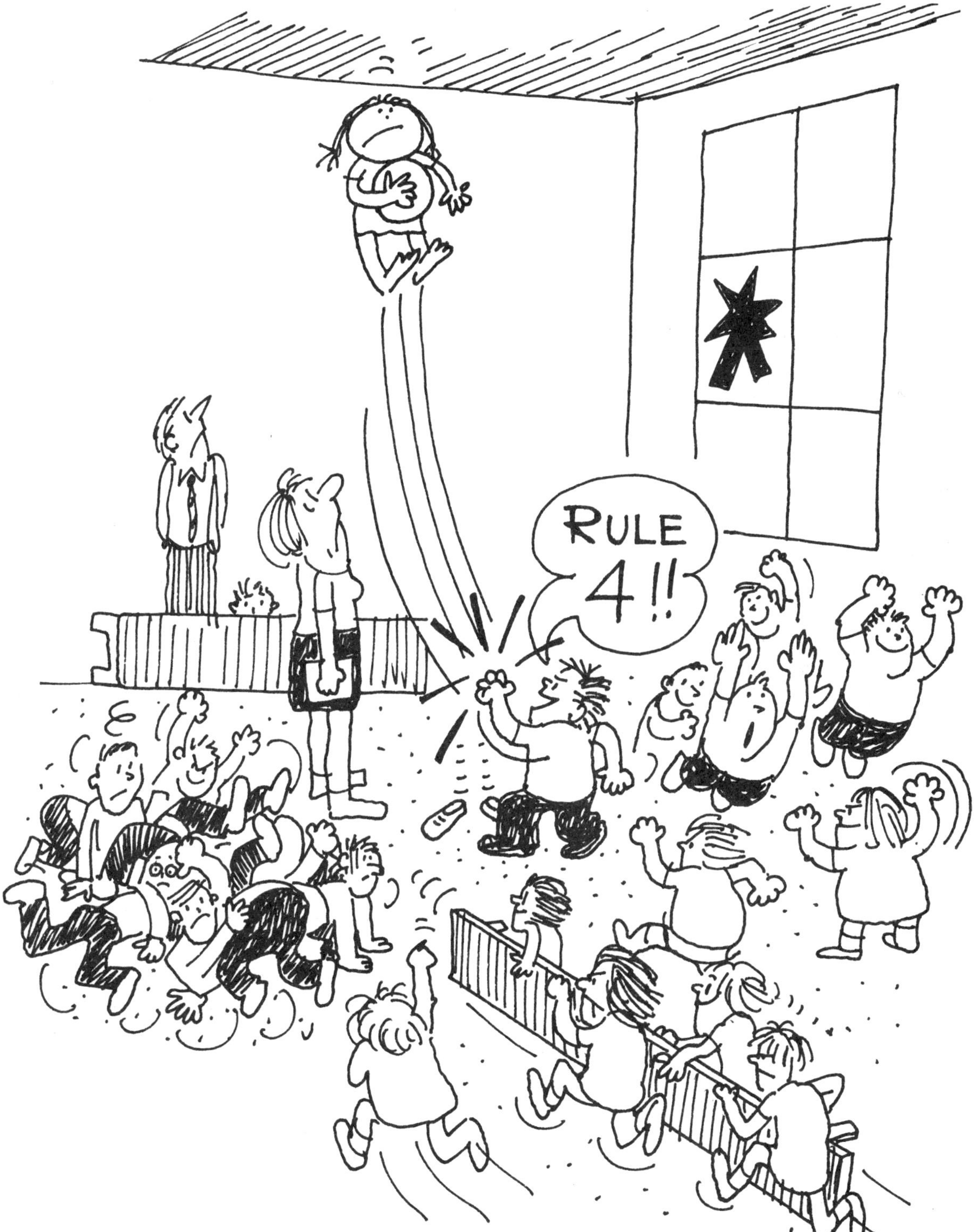
RULE 4!!

NON-STOP CRICKET

Time required
As appropriate but a minimum of 20 minutes, possibly 10 minutes for each innings.

Age range
8–13 years

Aim
To encourage teamwork and alertness.

Organisation
The whole class will be involved and the game can be played indoors in the hall or gym or outside in the playground or field.

Equipment
- a wicket of some sort (cricket stumps, box)
- a lightweight ball
- markers

Preparation
A pitch should be set out as shown. It may not be possible to have lines in which case some marker system must be used.

The class should be divided into two equal teams.

The batting side line up near the wicket.

The fielding side spread out to retrieve the ball and should include a back stop.

The first batsman stands in front of the wicket and a member of the fielding side (or the teacher) bowls.

Rules
1. The bowler bowls underarm and the batsman hits the ball with the palm of the hand.
2. To score, the batsman must run to B, touch the line with his foot and then run back to A. He continues to bat until he is given out.
3. The batsman must run whether he hits the ball or not.
4. Batsmen may wait at B until another ball has been bowled, but cannot then score a run.
5. The bowler must bowl continuously at the wicket and batsmen must be ready to face the bowler quickly. If a batsman is slow getting to the wicket he may be out before having a strike.
6. Batsmen are out if,
    - they are caught
    - they are bowled
    - they are touched with the ball (or hit by the ball providing the ball is soft) whilst running between A and B.

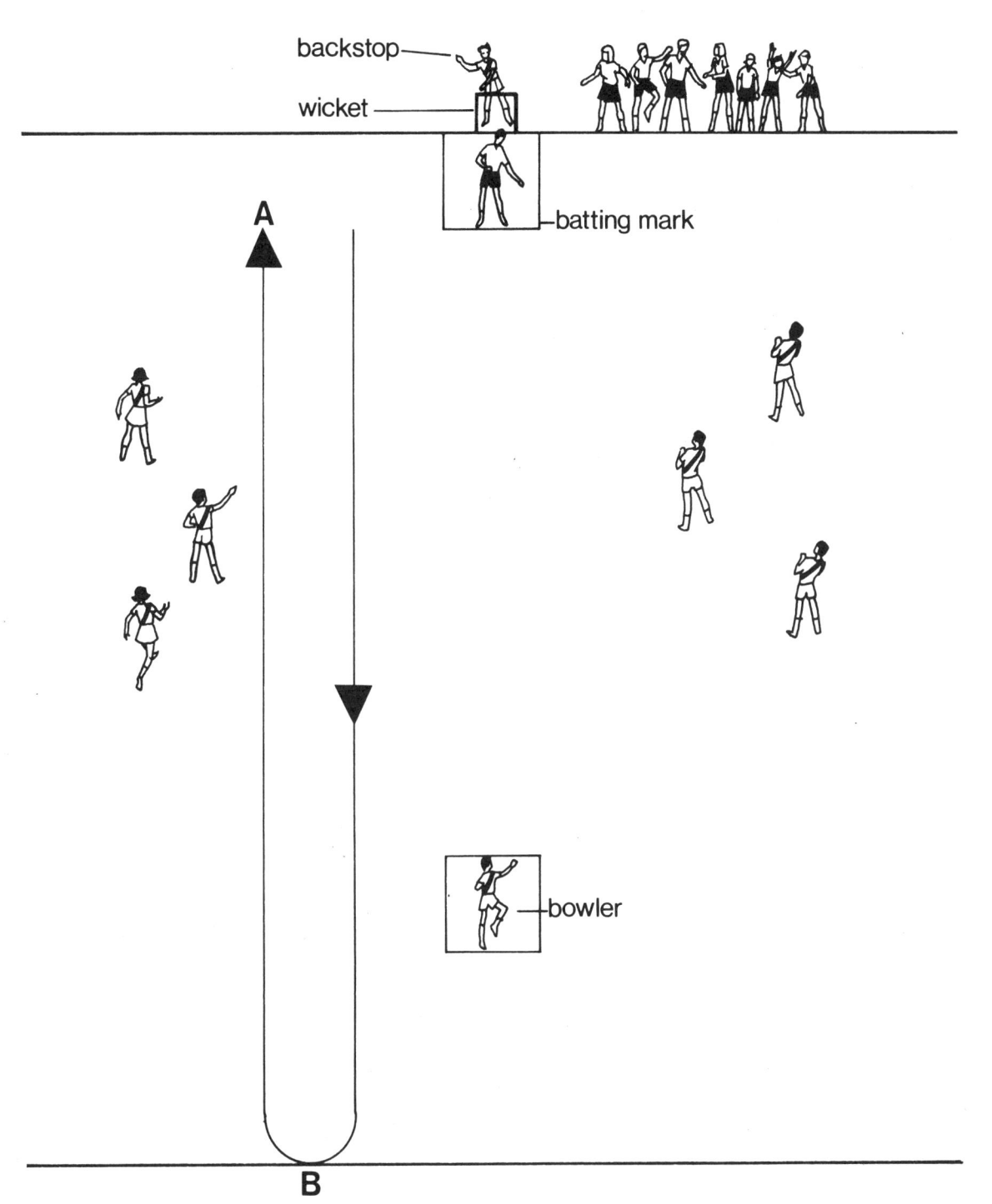

The game is made more exciting if a time limit is imposed on each innings or if the children have a target of a number of runs to score in a given time.

The Burglary

Background information
This lesson is divided into three stages:

1. The telling of the story by the teacher and the miming of the actions by the children. The story is told slowly, sentence by sentence, to give time for each event to be mimed.

2. The recalling, by the class, of all the details of the story.
   The teacher should sit the class down, and, by asking questions such as 'Where does the story begin?', 'What did the burglar do next?' and 'How far did he walk?', draw from the children *all* the details of the story in the correct order.

3. The re-enacting of the story by the children, *without* the teacher taking any part.
   This should include the children attaching their own ending to the story!

Time required
30–45 minutes

Age range
9–12 years

Aim
To develop the ability to recall information.

Organisation
This is a 'whole class' activity but each child will be working individually. It is necessary to use a hall or other large space, preferably with curtains or blinds closed to make the area as dimly lit as possible.

Equipment
Each child will need
> a chair

Discussion

Tell the children that they are going to mime a story as you read it to them. Explain that although the room will be crowded they must forget everyone else and imagine themselves alone.

Mention the fact that the chairs are only to sit on at the beginning of the lesson and that neither they, nor any other furniture or apparatus in the room should be used again during the story.

It may be advisable to tell the children that all noises, including creaks and groans should be imagined and not given voice. (This prevents concentration being broken, or laughter breaking out!)

Explain that a jemmy is a crowbar used by burglars for forcing windows open.

Further information and activities

1 This lesson is best used when the children have experience of other drama activities such as **Situations**, *see page* **34**. They are then less likely to be distracted or embarrassed.

2 Children could be encouraged to develop and mime situations of their own or perhaps to produce a story for the rest of the class to act out.

THE STORY to be read slowly, sentence by sentence. *See* **Background information** for lesson structure.

You are sitting in an armchair by the fire, reading a newspaper. You fold the newspaper and put it on the floor to the right of your chair. Looking at your watch, you note that the time is 9.23 pm. Getting up, you move to the right-hand side of the room, where there is a chest of drawers. Opening the bottom drawer you take out a small case and place it on top of the chest. You close the drawer and open the case. Inside, you check that the contents are in place – torch – screwdriver – jemmy – knife – glass cutter – rope – and hacksaw.

Close the case and carry it across the room to the door, which you open. Passing into the hall you put the case down while you take your coat from a peg on the wall. You put on your coat and then take your hat down from another peg and place that on your head. Picking up your case you walk the six steps to the door, which you undo, pass through and close behind you. Walking slowly to the front gate, you open it – it creaks and you decide that you must remember to oil it when you get back. Going through the gate you turn to the left and walk along the street until you get to the crossroads. (*Make this a longish pause to allow time for some walking.*)

At the crossroads you stop and look at your watch. The time is now 9.40 pm. Crossing the road carefully you carry on down the road to the right. You are now passing along a tree-lined avenue with large houses to your right. You stop by the big iron gates of a house and look around to see if anyone is watching. You walk quietly up the drive but the gravel crunches beneath your feet so you step quickly on to the lawn. You are walking along the grass verge at the edge of the drive when suddenly the front door of the house opens. You drop behind a bush and peer out cautiously. The door closes and while you watch, all the lights in the house go off. Standing up you walk carefully to the right-hand side of the house where you stop by a ground floor window. Placing your case on the ground you open it and take out the torch, which you place in your left-hand pocket, and your jemmy which you hold in your right hand. Leaving your case on the ground, you push the blade of the jemmy very carefully under the edge of the window. Trying to make as little noise as possible, you force the window and, after placing the jemmy on the ground, you push the window wide open. You take your torch from your pocket, switch it on and climb carefully over the window sill into the room. After pulling the window shut you take a plan from your pocket, open it up and shine the torch onto it. Looking round the room from the left you carefully check the items in the room with those marked on the plan – the door to the left – the table in the centre – the fireplace on the opposite wall – the painting on the wall above the fireplace – and the large safe door in the wall to the right. Carefully avoiding the table, you walk over to the safe. Placing your ear next to the lock, you turn the dials backwards and forwards until – suddenly the door opens smoothly and silently. Shining your torch into the safe you walk in and stand there looking around. On the shelves to the left you note piles of five-pound notes, in front of you jewels and to the right, bars of gold. You start to move towards the jewels when you hear a noise behind – you turn around quickly as the door closes with a bang. You dash to the door and push it, but it is firmly closed. As you stand wondering what to do you hear a humming noise and looking up you notice that the ceiling is gradually coming down towards you – down and down and . . .

(The children should now go back to their chairs – or sit on the floor, ready for stage 2).

It is not until stage 3 of the lesson that each child adds his or her own ending. These resolutions are likely to range from a merciful escape to a grisly, violent death or a slow and painful decline.

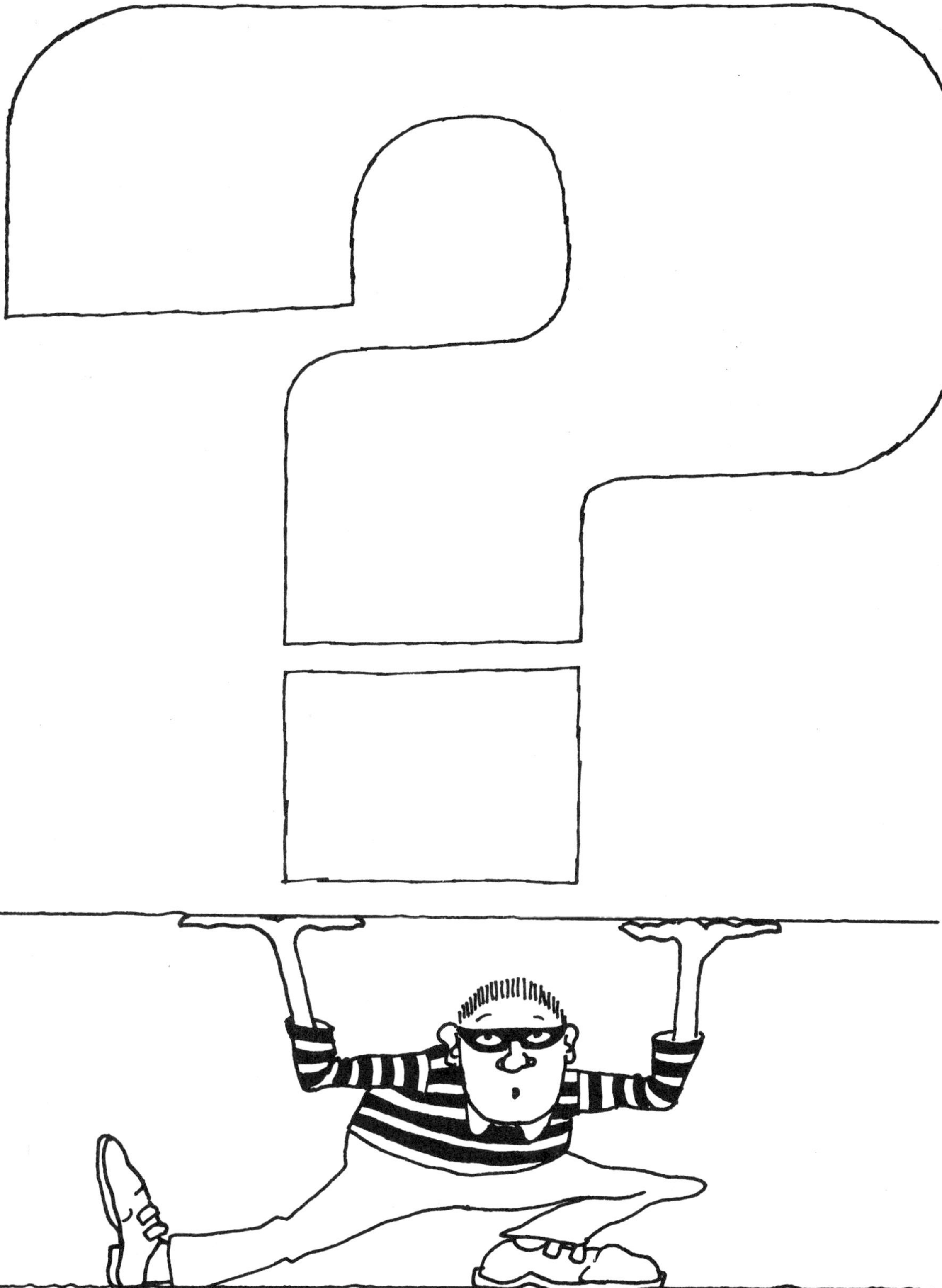

ship (sea going)	*circa* 7250 BC
potters wheel	*circa* 6500 BC
writing	*circa* 3400 BC
glass	*circa* 1500 BC
paper	*circa* 150 AD
windmill	*circa* 600 AD
spectacles	1289 AD
printing press	1455 AD

telescope	1608 AD
ship (steam)	1775 AD
locomotive	1804 AD
bicycle	1839 AD
aeroplane	1903 AD
television	1926 AD
hovercraft	1955 AD

WHEN?

Time required
30–40 minutes

Age range
10–13 years

Aim
To promote interest in the past and understanding of chronological order.

Organisation
Children should work in groups of 4 or more.

Equipment
Each group will need
> paper and pencil
>> (the teacher may like to have an encyclopaedia available, though this is not essential)

Background information
This lesson is based on some of the world's great inventions, and is basically a group discussion lesson. The following list contains 15 of the world's greatest inventions – each one being well separated in time from the others (with the exception of the most modern ones).

Preparation
The teacher should write the inventions on the blackboard omitting the dates and placing them in alphabetical order.

> aeroplane
> bicycle
> glass
> hovercraft
> locomotive
> paper
> potter's wheel
> printing press
> ship (sea going)
> ship (steam)
> spectacles
> telescope
> television
> windmill
> writing

Discussion
Talk to the children about inventions in general and use the following list as an introduction to the subject. These nine inventions, together with dates, will also have to be written on the blackboard.

maps	*circa* 2500 BC
solid wheel	*circa* 1900 BC
parchment	*circa* 1300 BC
mechanical clock	725 AD
watch	1462 AD
microscope	1590 AD
steam engine	1698 AD
manned balloon	1783 AD
car (petrol)	1885 AD

It will be necessary, and probably very valuable, to check the children's understanding of the BC/AD dating system during the discussion and to explain the significance of *circa* before a date.

Activity

Using these 9 inventions as pointers, each group should work out the order in which the 15 undated inventions came into being, starting with the earliest. Allow plenty of time for useful discussion within the groups before asking each group to write out the list in chronological order.

If the children are likely to enjoy an inter-group competition then a marking system can be used in which penalty points are scored for incorrect placings.

A correct position rates 0 points, one position out scores 1 penalty point, two positions out scores 2 penalty points and so on.

example

group order	correct order	points
1 writing	3rd	2
2 paper	5th	3
3 ship (sea-going)	1st	2
4 telescope	9th	5
5 glass	4th	1
6 windmill	6th	0

The group with the least number of penalty points is the winner. Using a scoring system has the advantage of promoting lots of general discussion as to how the children arrived at their decisions and consideration of the actual dates which can now be added to the list on the blackboard.

Further information and activities

This lesson could be used as an introduction to topics on inventions, transport or a particular period of history. It could also provide a useful means of checking the children's understanding of the BC/AD dating system.

DO NOT FEED THE ANIMALS

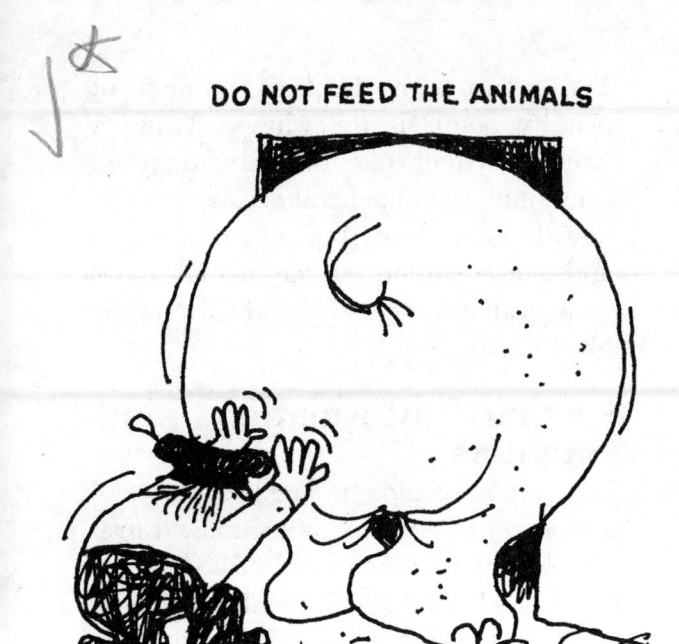

FILLING A ZOO

Time required
30 minutes.

Age range
8–11 years

Aim
To encourage children to think logically and to follow simple instructions.

Organisation
Children can work individually or in pairs if the teacher wishes to generate discussion leading to the correct solution.

Equipment
Each child will need
  paper and pencil

Background information
With a little thought the children should be able to fill the zoo by themselves, but the teacher may like to give them a start. There are 3 types of accommodation in the zoo:
  1 a bird and snake house
  2 12 individual pens each containing one type of animal
  3 2 'sociable' animal compounds, each containing 3 types of animal

Preparation
The teacher should draw the 'zoo' on the blackboard (leaving out the animals), and ask the children to copy it onto their paper, pointing out that some pens have trees (T), some have pools of water (W) and some have both.

Either dictate the directions to the children or write them on the blackboard.

Activity
Fill the zoo by using the following information (not necessarily in the order in which it is printed).
  1 Parrots can see out of the entrance.
  2 Snakes live between vultures and eagles.
  3 Elephants live with antelope.
  4 Eagles cannot see elephants.
  5 Sea-lions, polar bears, brown bears, penguins, tigers, wild boar, rhinoceroses and elephants need water pools.
  6 Zebra, monkeys, baboons, chimpanzees, brown bears, lions, tigers, leopards, pumas, wild boar and giraffes need trees.

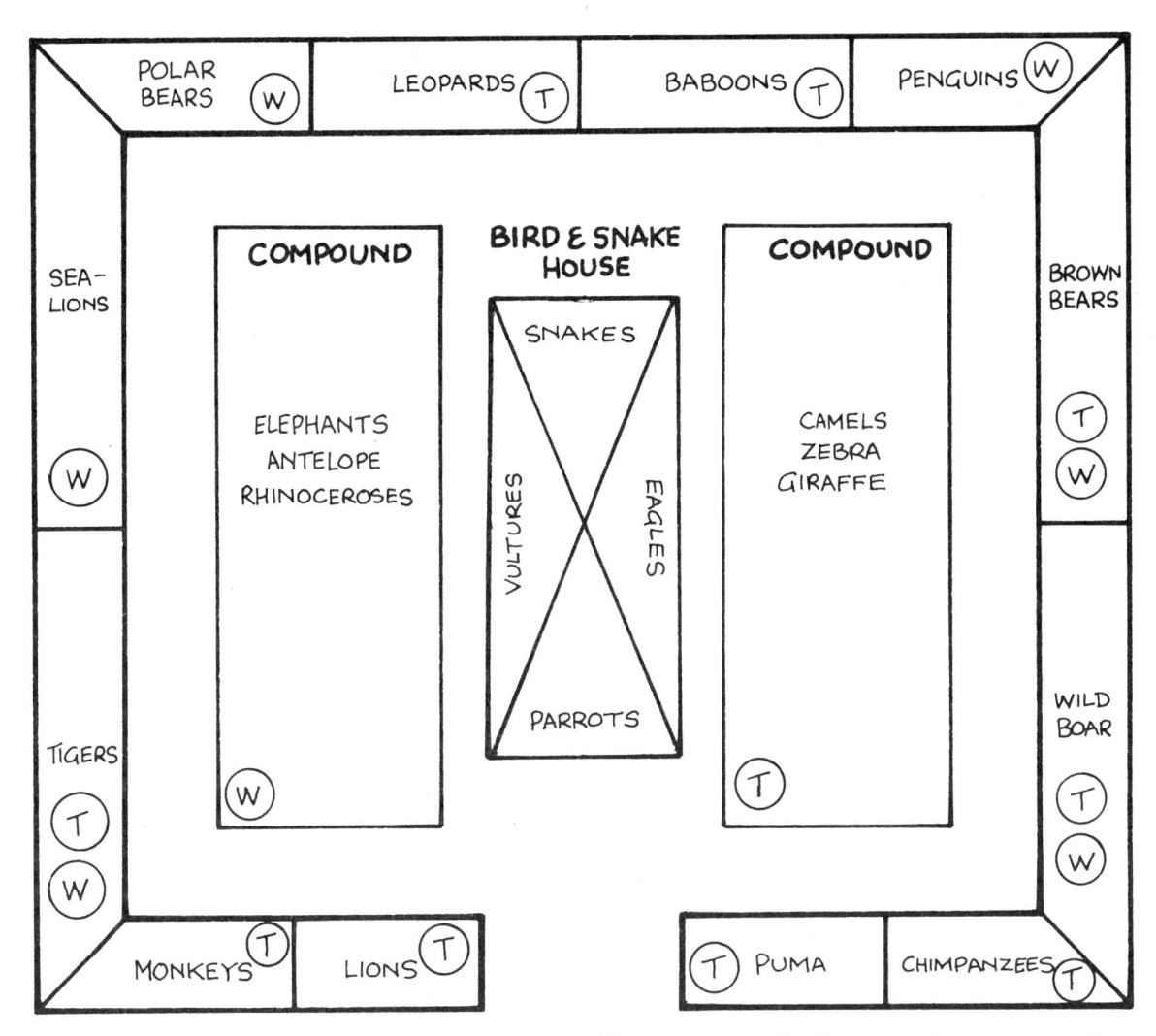

7 No two 'cats' live next to each other.
8 Camels live with zebra.
9 No two members of the 'monkey' family live next to each other.
10 Tigers live between sea-lions and monkeys.
11 Sea-lions live next to polar bears.
12 Wild boar live between brown bears and chimpanzees.
13 Baboons live between leopards and penguins.
14 Lions live nearer to monkeys than to chimpanzees.

Further information and activities

1 The teacher may want to start with a much simplified version, especially with younger children.
2 Older children may wish to produce a grid and instructions on their own, to be tested by others in the class. A museum, a shopping precinct, a seating plan or a planting scheme are all possible subjects for such an exercise.
3 The lesson could be used before a zoo visit.

FLOW DIAGRAM

Time required
30 minutes

Age range
10–13 years

Aim
To use a flow diagram to describe a simple operation.

Organisation
Children to work individually.

Equipment
Each child will need
- a piece of paper, at least A4 size to allow plenty of scope
- a pen or pencil
- a ruler

Background information
Flow diagrams are being used increasingly in all kinds of work including organisation, instruction, description and fault-finding. A flow diagram should be far easier to understand than a page of written information.

Preparation
Draw the following flow diagram on the blackboard, either before the children come into the classroom, or draw it and explain it as part of the discussion. Alternatively it may be useful to produce your own flow diagram and hand out duplicated sheets for the children to follow during the discussion.

Discussion
Talk about the flow diagram. Ask the children to suggest possible operations or situations for which a flow diagram could be created. Tell the children that flow diagrams should begin with START and end with FINISH.

All <u>instruction</u> boxes are rectangle in shape.

All <u>decision</u> boxes are diamond-shaped.

Activity
Ask the children to produce their own flow diagram for one of these operations.
- laying the table
- putting out a piece of P.E. equipment
- serving school dinners
- washing the car

or for one of the operations suggested during the preliminary discussion.

Further activities
This lesson could be the first in a series of lessons investigating different methods of presenting information.

Flowchart 1

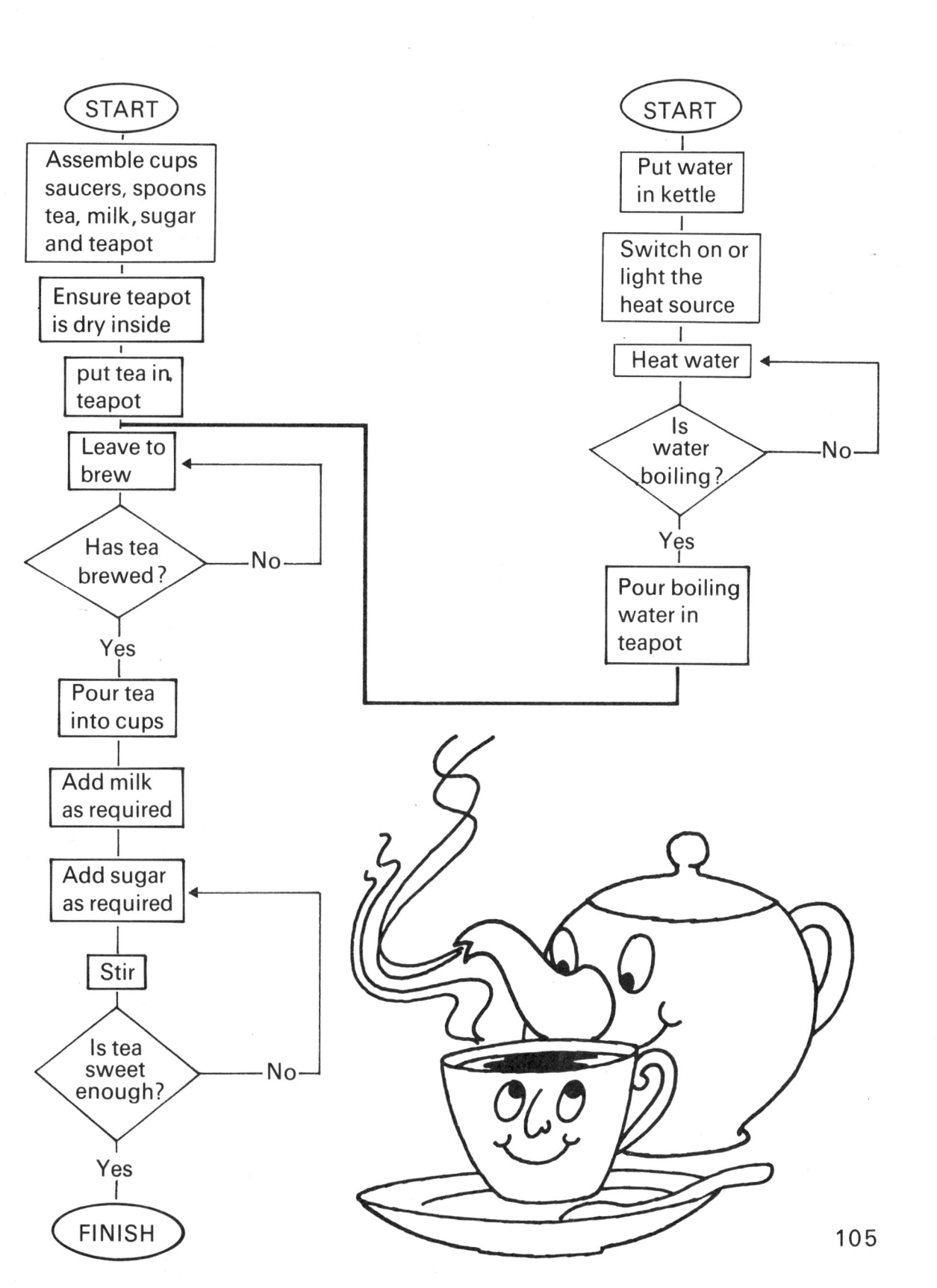

START
↓
Assemble cups, saucers, spoons, tea, milk, sugar and teapot
↓
Ensure teapot is dry inside
↓
put tea in teapot
↓
Leave to brew ←──────────┐
↓   │
Has tea brewed? ──No──────┘
↓ Yes
Pour tea into cups
↓
Add milk as required
↓
Add sugar as required ←───┐
↓   │
Stir   │
↓   │
Is tea sweet enough? ──No──┘
↓ Yes
FINISH

Flowchart 2

START
↓
Put water in kettle
↓
Switch on or light the heat source
↓
Heat water ←──────────┐
↓   │
Is water boiling? ──No─┘
↓ Yes
Pour boiling water in teapot
↓
(connects to "Leave to brew" in Flowchart 1)

Survival

Time required
30 minutes

Age range
10–13 years

Aim
To plan a survival kit.

Organisation
The children may work individually or in pairs.

Equipment
Each child will need
     paper and pencil

Background information
The lesson is concerned with the means of surviving in hostile, outdoor conditions. Any one of us may suddenly at some time in our lives be plunged into an emergency situation — becoming lost, an air crash, or a blizzard where survival is all important. The basic requirement in such a situation, however desperate, is the will to survive — the will to live.

Discussion
Begin by talking to the children about the situations where a person might find himself in difficulties.

Try to elicit from the children the basic requirements for survival in such circumstances — these apply whenever and wherever the emergency occurs.

They may be listed simply as:

1. The will to survive
2. Protection
3. Warmth
4. Food
5. Water
6. First Aid
7. Aids to discovery

If the teacher had knowledge of first aid it would be useful to discuss with the children:

a) means of stopping bleeding
b) treatment of shock
c) how to immobilise a fracture
d) protection and cleaning of wounds.

Activity
Ask the children to devise for themselves a personal survival kit (not bigger than a cocoa tin) bearing in mind the criteria listed above.

When they have all completed their lists of contents a further discussion should take place as to what they have in their tins and why.

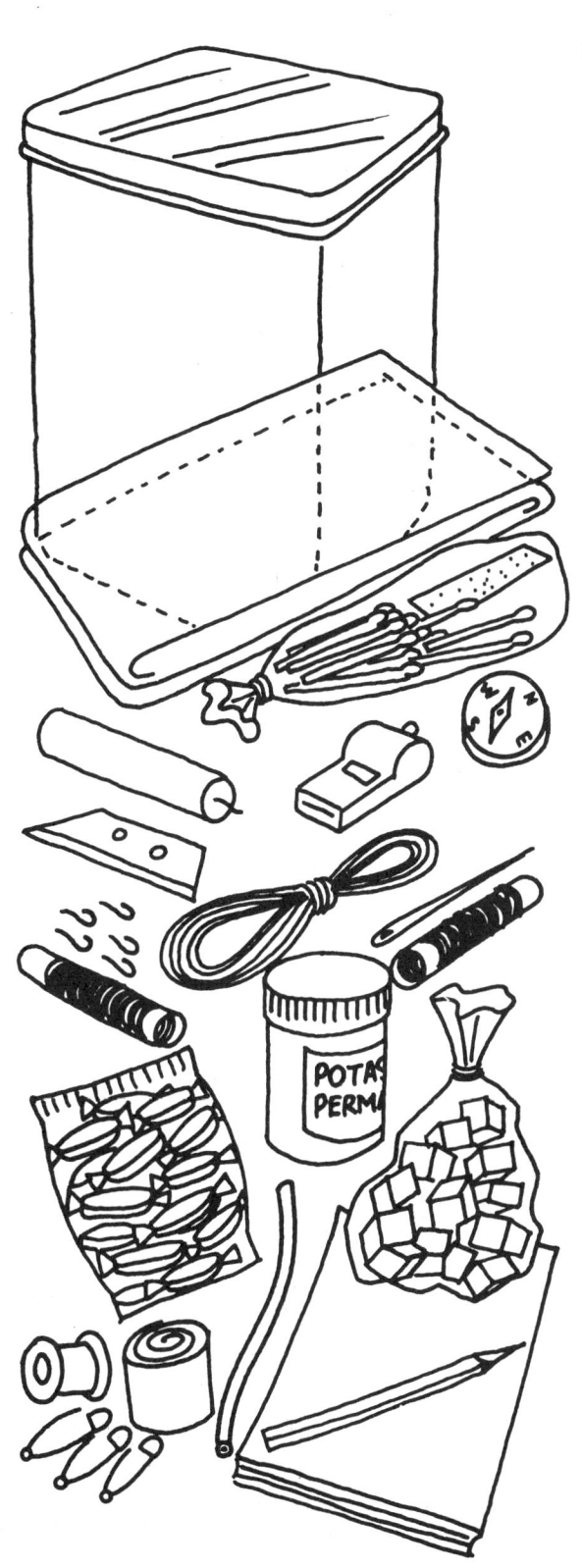

Suggested contents

1. The container should be a tin such as a cocoa or tobacco tin (because they are easy to make watertight), with a highly reflective lid (used for reflecting the sun as a signal).
2. A large polythene bag – to sit in for protection in cold or at night (with head outside of course).
3. Matches & striker from side of matchbox – heads of matches dipped in wax and, along with striker, placed in a small plastic bag bound tightly with insulation tape.
4. A small candle – for use as a firelighter.
5. A small, shrill whistle.
6. A small magnetic compass.
7. A single-edged razor blade or sharp pocket knife.
8. String.
9. Needle and stout thread for repairs to clothes.
10. Fishing line, and hooks.
11. Crystals of Potassium Permanganate – useful for purifying water and as an antiseptic as well as being a red marker dye when mixed with snow or water.
12. Glucose sweets.
13. Sugar lumps (in plastic bag) to eat or to help light a fire.
14. Plasters, bandage, a piece of gauze and some safety pins.
15. Notepaper and pencil.
16. A piece of rubber tubing (to suck water from leaves or amongst rocks etc).

The Tower of Hanoi

Demonstration
Place the tins at point A, the smaller tin on top of the larger, and then rebuild the pile at point C, never putting the larger tin on top of the smaller one.

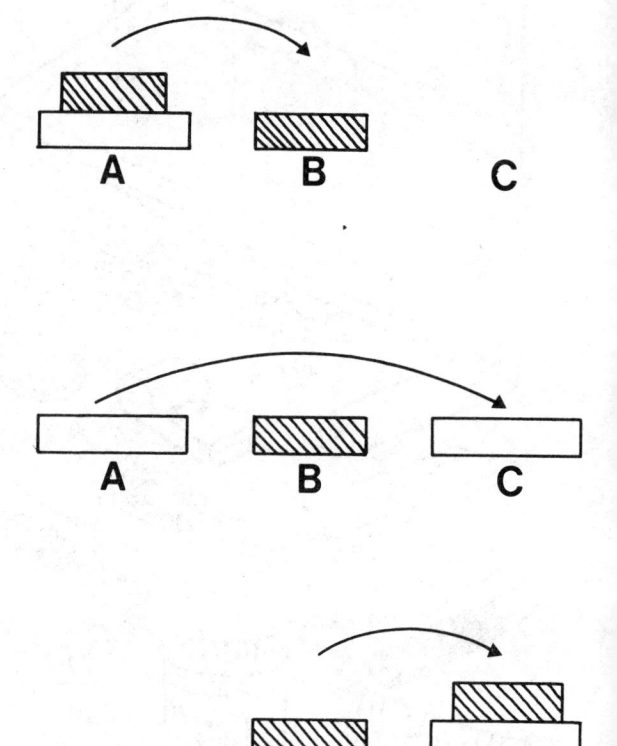

Time required
20 minutes

Age range
9–13 years

Aim
To explore logical sequences.

Organisation
Children can work individually or in pairs.

Equipment
The teacher will need two round tins or similar objects of different sizes.

Each child will need four flat objects of different sizes – suitable items are:
round tins, counters, coins, draughts, flat rubbers, weights etc.

paper and pencil

Ask the children how many moves were used to rebuild the pile of tins at C. They will have no difficulty in understanding that this exercise requires 3 moves.

Activity 1

Ask the children to make a pile of three different sized tins (or objects) and rebuild it at point C, moving only one tin at a time and never putting a larger object on top of a smaller one.

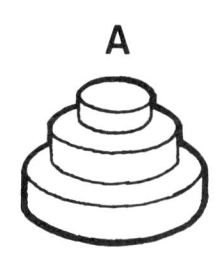

A

B

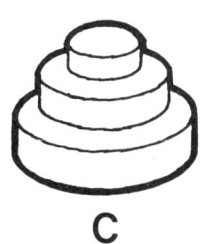

C

Note: Use only 3 points throughout, A B C

Discussion

Find out which child can rebuild the pile with the least number of moves. It can in fact be done in 7 moves.

Activity 2

Now ask the class to try with four tins. The least number of moves is 15. At this point some children will realise that there is a correlation between number of tins and number of moves. Some children may want to try five tins (or objects) which is fine if time allows, but if the results already noted are placed in the following table and written up on the blackboard the least number of moves can be worked out mathematically. By doubling the previous number of moves and adding one, the following table can be produced.

No. of tins	No. of moves
2	3
3	7
4	15
5	31
6	63
7	127
8	255
9	511
10	1023

Further activities

This lesson could be extended to an exploration of other games and puzzles. Many libraries have books on the subject, often in the mathematics section and it is fascinating to create up-to-date versions of well known puzzles. A game in a book, however well illustrated, is a poor substitute for the model which can be made and handled by the children themselves.

EYES

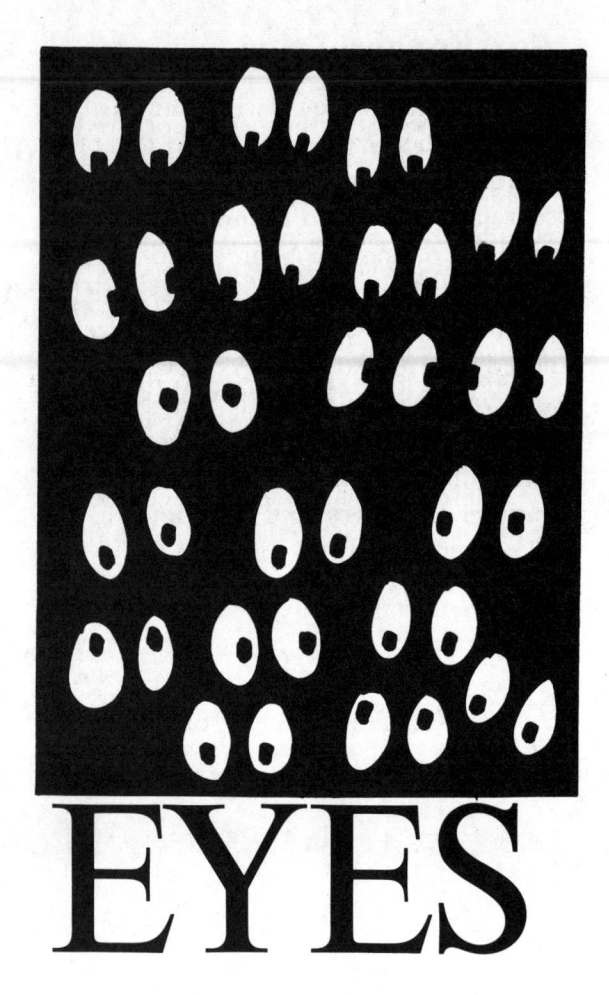

Background information

This lesson is based on a few very simple experiments aimed at demonstrating the functions and restrictions of the human eye. The eye is a roughly spherical mass which bulges slightly at the front. It is joined *via* the optic nerve to the brain. It is filled with a jelly-like substance known as vitreous humour.

side view

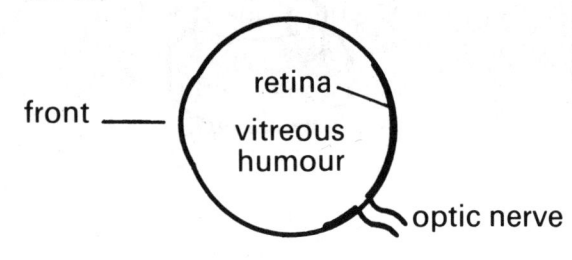

The innermost layer (or skin) is the light-sensitive layer known as the retina.

front view

The iris (covered by cornea)

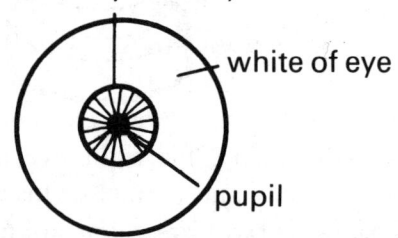

Light rays pass through the pupil (a hole) and strike the retina where the 'picture' is formed.

The iris contracts or expands depending upon the amount of light, thus making the pupil larger or smaller.

Time required
30 minutes

Age range
8–11 years

Aim
To observe eye functions.

Organisation
Children should work in pairs.

Equipment
Each pair of children will need
- 2 pencils
- 2 pieces of paper

Discussion

Talk about the eye and its parts with the children.

Activities

1 The children should look at each other's eyes, one at a time and identify the various visible parts *ie* the white (sclerotic layer), the iris (coloured part), and the pupil.
2 One child from each pair should sit down facing the window, and cover one of his eyes completely with his hand. After about 15 seconds the child should remove his hand quickly whilst the second child observes the eye closely.

What happens to the pupil?
(It will have got much larger in the darkness and will contract rapidly when the hand is taken away.)

What happens slowly in the next few seconds?
(The eye will settle down gradually and the pupil will slowly enlarge to its former size.)

3 Using both his eyes, each child should line up a pencil with some vertical line such as a window frame. He should then close his right eye and open it again – and then close his left eye. The pencil will appear to jump sharply to one side when one of the eyes is closed. The eye which is closed when the pencil 'jumps' is the one which is 'dominant'. When the pencil is being lined up with the vertical line this is the eye which makes the alignment although both eyes seem to be used.

Further activities

1 One child holds a pencil in front of partner. The other child opens and closes alternate eyes whilst looking at the pencil. His partner will seem to jump from side to side.
2 Draw a thick cross and black spot about 10 cm apart on a piece of paper. Move the paper away from the eyes with the left eye closed. Look hard at the X and the black spot will disappear when the light rays from it fall on the 'blindspot'. (There are no light-sensitive cells where the optic nerve leaves the retina and goes to the brain.)
3 Do a survey of eye colours.

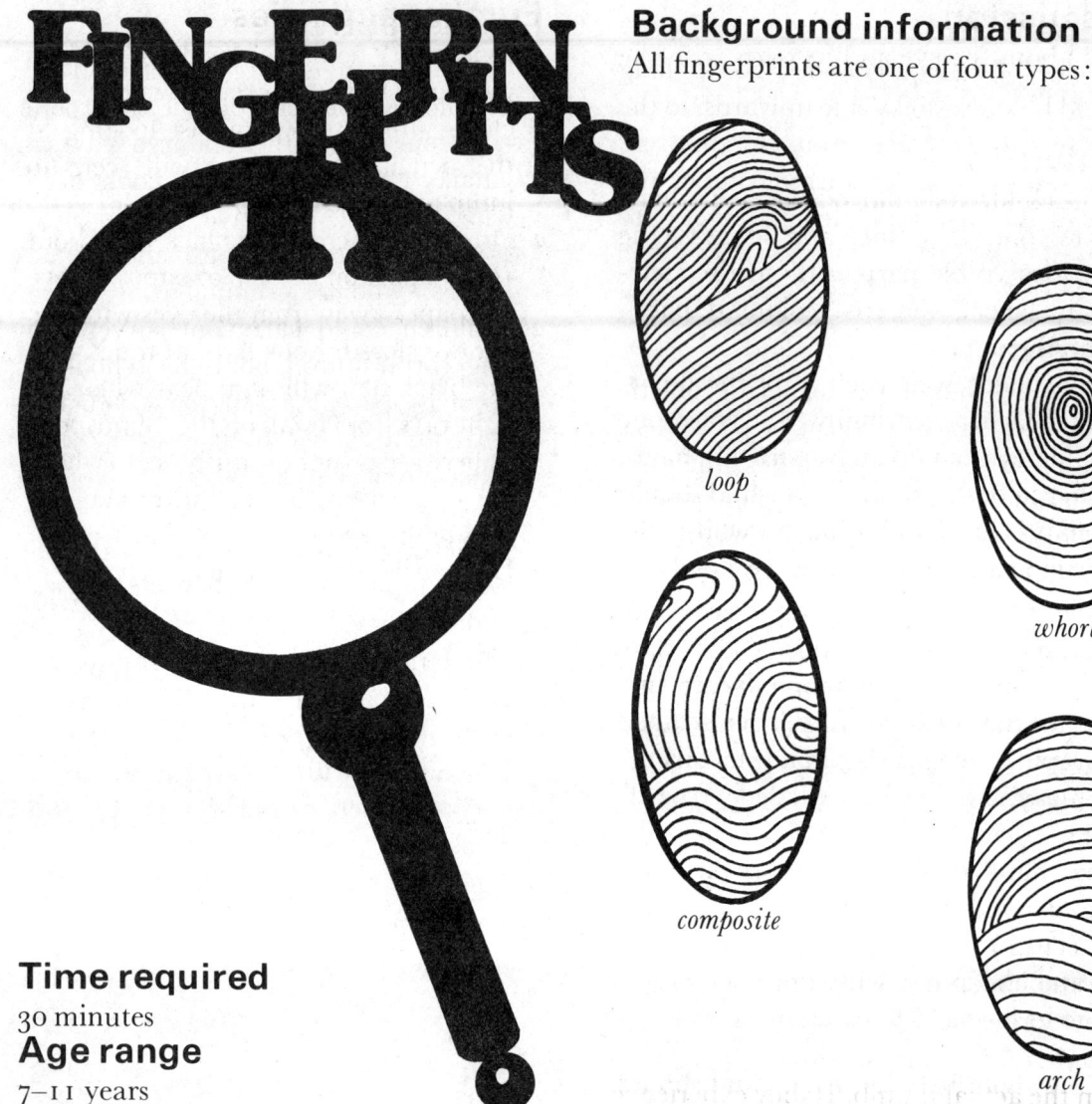

FINGERPRINTS

Background information
All fingerprints are one of four types:

loop

whorl

composite

arch

Time required
30 minutes

Age range
7–11 years

Aim
To discover the four different types of fingerprints.

Organisation
Children to work in groups of 4–6.

Equipment
- a roll of sellotape (for use by teacher)
- white chalk (one piece for each group)
- plain paper and a pencil for each child

These types may be found in any combination on any hand. No two people have ever been known to have identical fingerprints – they are even slightly different in identical twins. Fingerprints taken by Scotland Yard have been shown to consist of approximately 60% loops, 5% arches, 35% whorls and composites.

In a class of 35 – you might therefore expect to have approximately 21 loops, 2 arches and 12 whorls and composites in a survey of all right-hand index fingers.

Preparation

A piece of sellotape about 20 cm long should be stuck sticky side upwards, to the desk or table of each group of children. This can be done by turning under the ends of the strip and sticking them onto the table.

Activity 1

Draw the four types of print on the blackboard or large sheet of paper. Ask each child to chalk one finger (the same finger for each child) and then press it carefully on to the sellotape strip. This should leave a good print on the sellotape which the children can examine in detail. Each group should now decide how many of the prints in their group fall into each category and a class tally can be taken. Whether or not this is compared with the Scotland Yard analysis will depend on the children's understanding of percentages.

Activity 2

Ask the children to draw, on the piece of paper provided, the pattern of their left thumb – this should be done much larger than the actual thumb. If they experience difficulty in discerning the pattern, let them chalk over their thumbs. The pattern will then stand out more clearly. Obviously left-handed children will have to draw the pattern of their right thumbs.

Further activities

1 One child in each group should be blindfolded or sent out of the room while one of the other children leaves a 'chalky' fingerprint on a book or a window. The 'detective' should then come back to the group and try to discover who the 'criminal' is.
2 Children could carry out surveys on fingerprints throughout the school or amongst parents. Can they find any correlation between fingerprints and other physical attributes such as colour of eyes?
3 Fingerprints can be 'lifted' with sellotape from solid surfaces such as desks and windows.
4 The large thumbprint drawings could form the basis of some attractive artwork or could be exploited for language work with descriptive words or poems written within the whorls and loops.
5 The lesson could be used as an introduction to a topic on the police.

See **Further Activities** 4.

PAPER AEROPLANES

Time required
20 minutes

Age range
9–13 years

Aim
To investigate certain aspects of aeroplanes and flight.

Organisation
Children should work individually. This lesson could be taken in the hall or gym where there is plenty of floor area for the children to make their aeroplanes and plenty of space for flight practice and competition.

Equipment
It would be useful if the teacher had a roll of sellotape handy, some paper clips and possibly a pair of scissors.

Each child will need
pieces of paper (minimum size 220 mm × 175 mm – maximum 280 mm × 215 mm)

Background information
The wings of an aeroplane give it <u>lift</u> when air pushes on them from underneath. We can demonstrate this and other simple principles of flight by making paper aeroplanes. Forward movement of an aeroplane is called <u>thrust</u> – this is usually provided by engines but with a paper aeroplane it is provided by the thrower.

LIFT and THRUST are the favourable forces acting on an aeroplane but counteracting these we have GRAVITY, or WEIGHT (pulling downwards) and DRAG (against forward movement by the pressure of air on wings and fuselage).

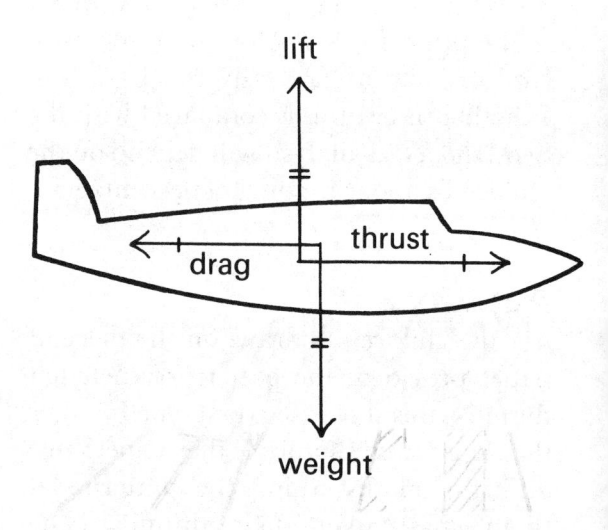

FLAPS are used on wings to give more lift. STABILIZERS are used to steady the flight.

Discussion
Talk to the children about the way air is used to give lift to an aeroplane and about the forces acting against it.

Preparation

The teacher should make a 'standard' paper aeroplane in front of the class as follows:

1. Fold piece of paper in half lengthways and then fold two corners down towards the centre (fig. 1).
2. Fold in the two sides again towards the centre along the dotted line (fig. 2). Make sure all creases are sharp.

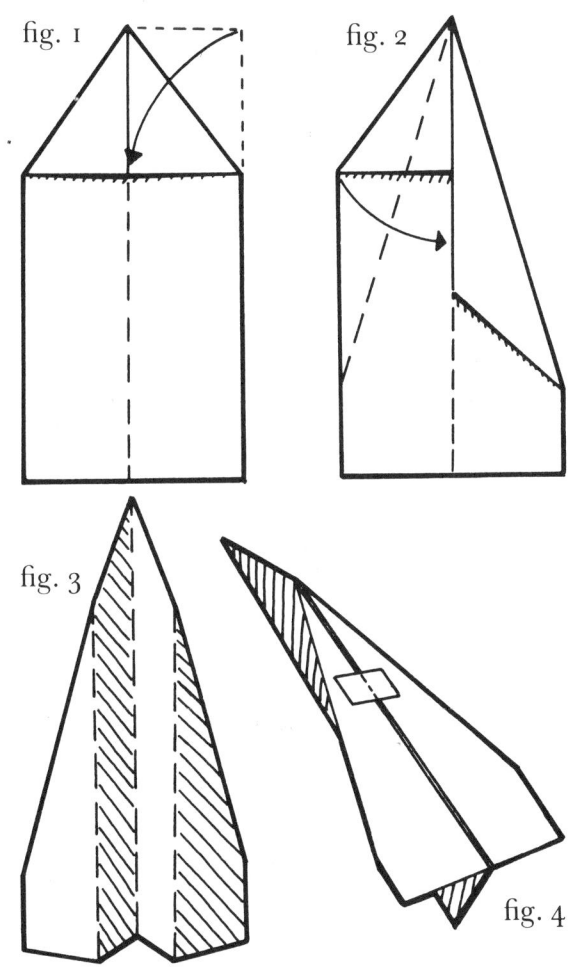

fig. 1

fig. 2

fig. 3

fig. 4

3. Turn the aeroplane over and fold the two wings back along a crease about 1½–2 cm from the centre fold (fig. 3).
4. Press down firmly on all creases.
5. Turn the aeroplane over again and join the wings with a small piece of sellotape (fig. 4).

Throw the aeroplane and then show by turning up the edges of the wings (about 1 cm) how the flight can be stabilized. You can also cut or tear small flaps on the rear edges of the wings and, by bending them slightly, achieve different degrees of lift.

Activity

Let the children develop their own paper aeroplanes and carry out test flights, either in classroom or gym, or outside if not too windy. The designs need not be as conventional as the demonstration model, but you could say that you are looking for three 'best' aeroplanes:

   a) the one that gives the longest flight
   b) the most aerobatic
   c) the most unusual (as long as it flies)

Further activities

This lesson could be used as a basis for work on air or to introduce a topic on flight. Kites could be designed and tested.

Reactions

Time required
20 minutes

Age range
9–12 years

Aim
To carry out a simple scientific experiment with standardised measurement.

Organisation
Children will need to work in pairs.

Equipment
- a stopwatch or a watch with a second hand for teacher's use only

Each pair of children will need
- a rule or stick measured in centimetres
- a piece of paper
- a pencil

Background information
It has been measured that the fastest messages from the nervous system of a human being travel at 388 kmh. In practice it is probably impossible for a human to react to a stimulus in less than 1/10th of a second – this is the time within which a false start is recorded with electric timing devices in many International Athletic meetings.

This lesson is to test reactions by getting the child to grasp a rule or measuring stick dropped by another without warning. An object accelerates towards the earth at approximately 9.81 m per sec^2 (32.17 ft per sec^2). This means that the following table can be used to measure the children's reactions:

$$5 \text{ cm} = 1/10\text{th second}$$
$$19.5 \text{ cm} = 2/10\text{ths second}$$
$$44 \text{ cm} = 3/10\text{ths second}$$
$$78.5 \text{ cm} = 4/10\text{ths second}$$

In other words, if a child manages to catch a metre stick or a ruler at approximately the 19.5 cm mark (see diagram below) he has reacted in approximately 2/10ths of a second.

Discussion
The teacher should discuss briefly with the children acceleration due to Earth's gravity, pointing out that in the first second of free fall an object will drop approximately 4.90 m. In the second second it will fall 14.72 m, so that at the end of the second second it will have fallen 4.90 m + 14.72 m = 19.62 m and it will continue accelerating at this rate until it hits the ground. The effect of air resistance will depend on the density and shape of the object dropped.

Activity

One child in each pair should hold the rule or stick so that the zero mark is level with the top of the loosely clenched hand of the other child, thus:

Note: The hand should be held so that there is plenty of room for the rule to drop through cleanly.

The child holding the rule then, without any warning, lets it go. The child who is being tested grabs the rule as quickly as possible and holds it firmly so that the measurement can be taken. The mark nearest the top of the hand is taken.

19.5 cm gives a reaction time of approximately 2/10ths of a second.

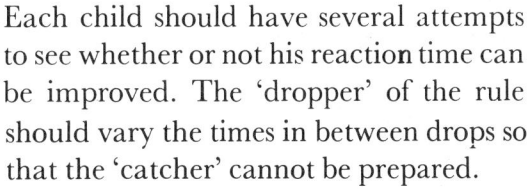

Each child should have several attempts to see whether or not his reaction time can be improved. The 'dropper' of the rule should vary the times in between drops so that the 'catcher' cannot be prepared.

Careful recording of results will demonstrate whether reaction times improve or whether, after a time, they worsen through carelessness or tiredness.

Further information and activities

1 Graphs could be made to show improved (or worsening) reactions.
2 Children in a class can stand in a circle holding hands. The teacher joins in the circle and starts a 'chain reaction' by squeezing the hand of the person on his or her left, at the same time starting the watch. As soon as the next person feels the squeeze he should squeeze the hand of the person on his left, and so on. When the 'squeeze' arrives back at the teacher he stops the watch. An average reaction time can then be worked out for each member of the class. Trying to improve on the time is interesting, but care should be taken that no one is watching for the squeeze in anticipation!

Magic square solution

See page **60**

1. The number 1 is always placed in the centre of the top row.
2. Each successive number is placed in the square diagonally upwards and to the right <u>if this is possible.</u> THIS IS THE GENERAL RULE.
3. If the next number would have to be placed <u>above</u> the top row then it is placed in the square at the very bottom of the column it would have gone in.

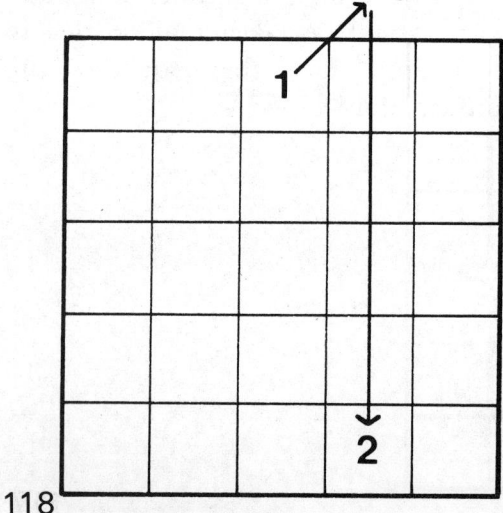

4. If the next consecutive number would have to be placed <u>outside</u> the right-hand column then it is placed in the square on the extreme left-hand side of the row it would have gone in.

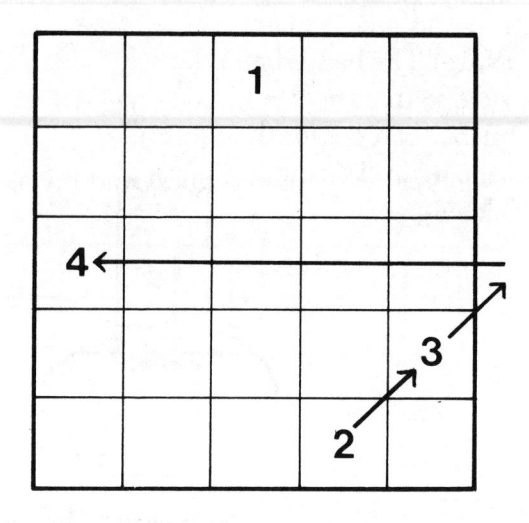

5. If the next number is blocked by another number, or the top right-hand corner of the square, then it is placed in the square immediately below the previous number.

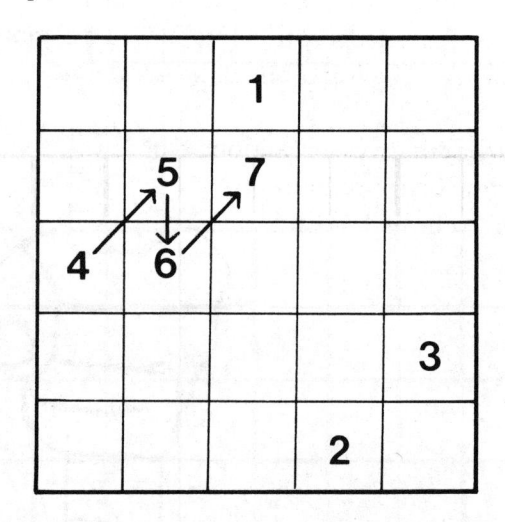

For the completed square, *see example a,* page **60**

Solution to Pentomino puzzle

See page **82**

If you tried placing the 12 pentominoes in line, there are over sixty thousand million million combinations. At one piece per second, it would take over 20 billion years to exhaust all the possible permutations!

There are only 2 solutions. The second one involves the removal of the two ends (as indicated by dotted lines) and reversing them.

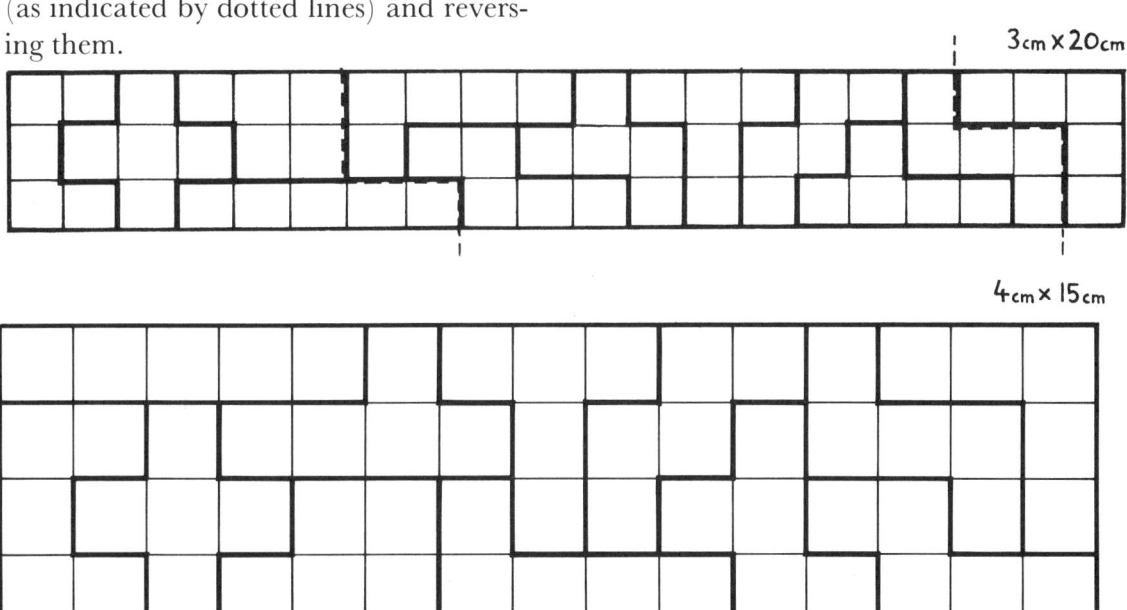

3cm × 20cm

4cm × 15cm

6cm × 10cm

119

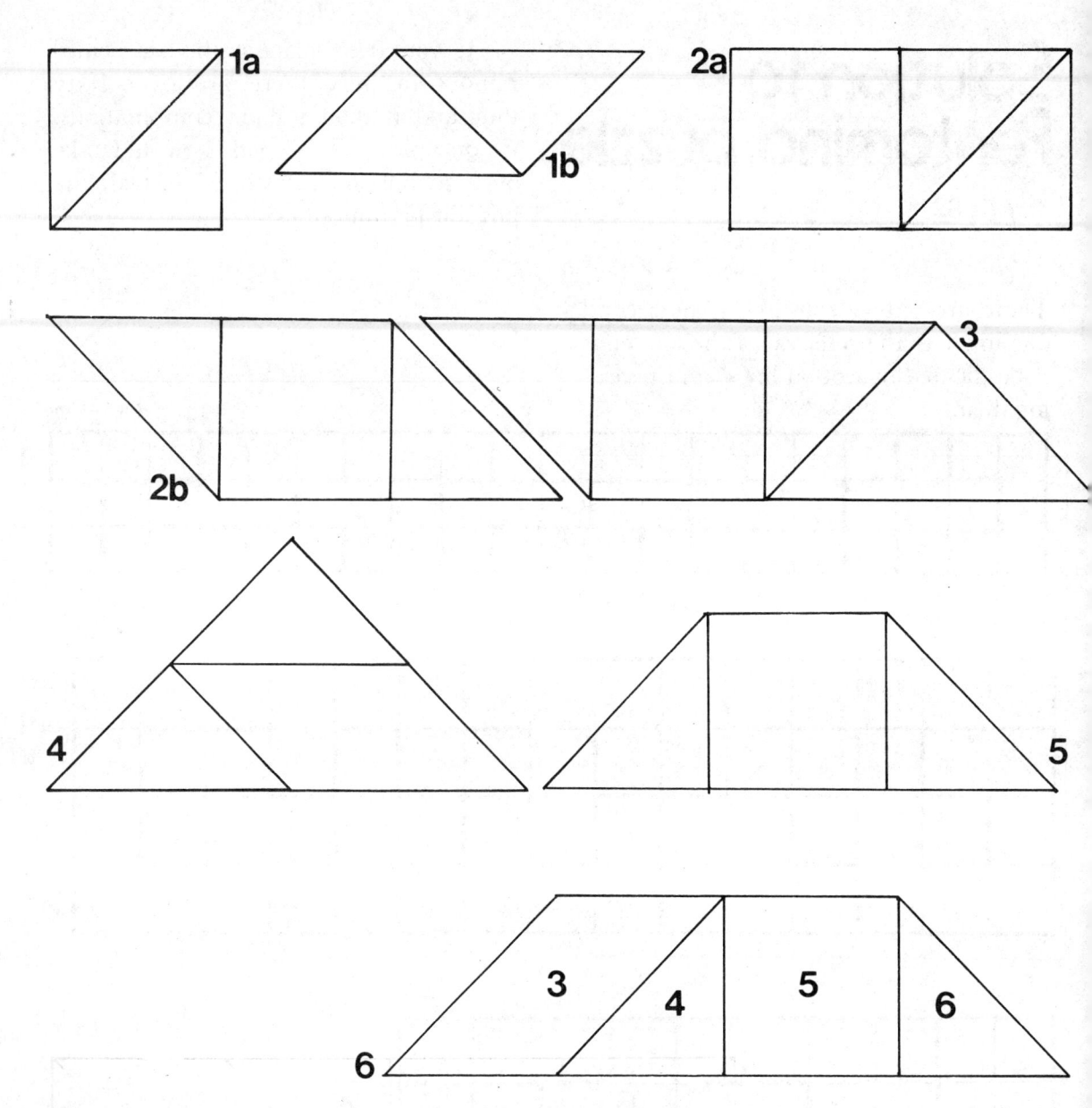

Solutions to Tangrams constructions

See page **84**.

One example only has been given for each construction. There are often many possible ways of forming the various figures.

7

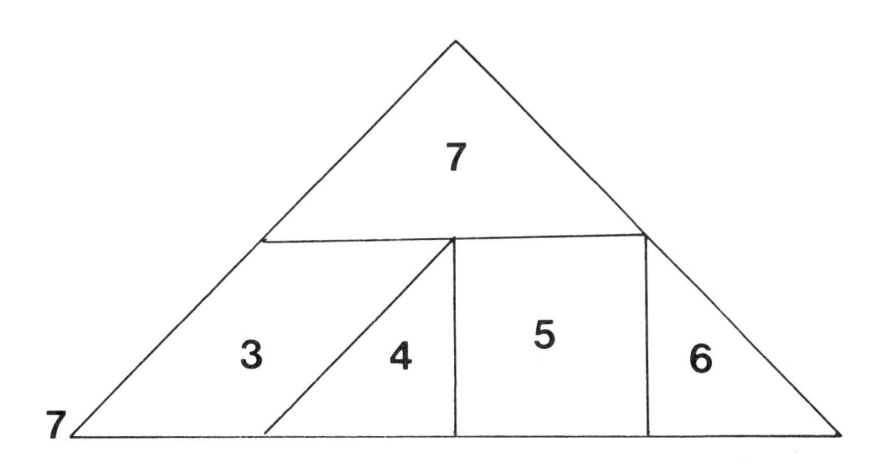

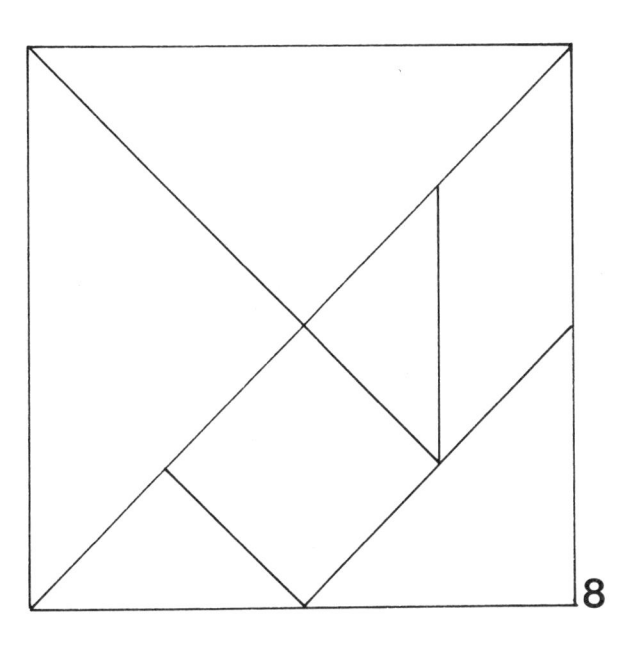

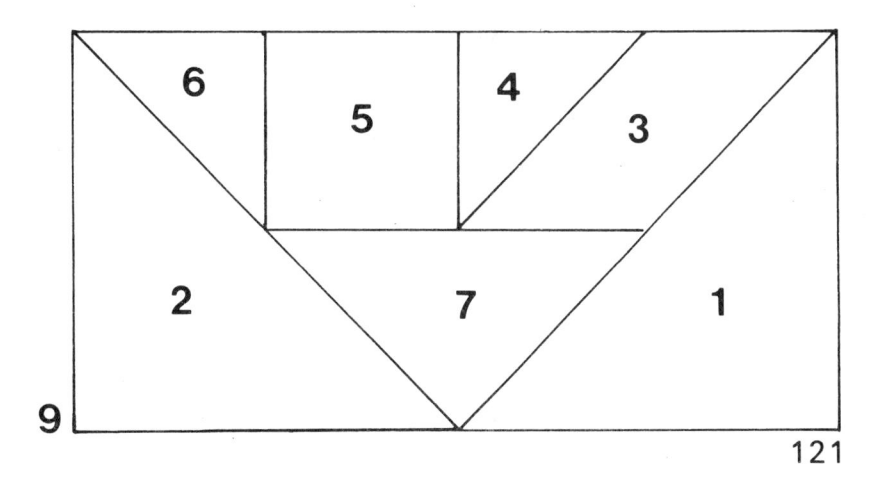

3 4 5 6

7

8

6 5 4 3
2 7 1
9
121

Lesson notes

Use these pages for your own stand-by lessons